Live from the Trenches

Live
from the Trenches

The Changing Role
of the Television News
Correspondent

Edited by Joe S. Foote

With a Foreword by
Ted Koppel

Southern Illinois University Press
Carbondale and Edwardsville

Copyright © 1998 by the Board of Trustees, Southern Illinois University
All rights reserved
Printed in the United States of America

01 00 99 98   4 3 2 1

Library of Congress Cataloging-in-Publication Data
Live from the trenches : the changing role of the television news
    correspondent / edited by Joe S. Foote ; with a foreword by Ted
Koppel.
        p.   cm.
    Contributions by correspondents; includes the discussion held during
    a conference at Southern Illinois University at Carbondale, Apr. 1996.

    1. Television broadcasting of news—United States. 2. Television
        journalists—United States—Biography. I. Foote, Joe S.
    PN4784.T4L594 1998
    070.1'95—dc21
                                                        98-18376
    ISBN 0-8093-2232-3 (cloth : alk. paper)   CIP

The paper used in this publication meets the minimum requirements of
American National Standard for Information Sciences—Permanence
of Paper for Printed Library Materials, ANSI Z39.48-1984. ∞

Contents

Foreword

It is not the role or the importance of reporters that is changing, it is the number. Also, it is the reach and the access available to those who would report the events of our times that has changed. If we want to understand the impact of our rapidly changing technology, it may help to revisit, however briefly, the environment in which American journalism is committed. What does it take to be a reporter in America? Nothing. Who has the right to call himself a reporter in America? Everyone. That is both the bane and the glory of the First Amendment. We require a license of a plumber. We need a license to fish or to drive, but anyone can be a journalist. It requires neither permission, nor validation, nor even an education.

Until fairly recently, that was of greater theoretical than practical importance; certainly when it came to television journalism. When I first joined ABC News in the summer of 1963, we worked with film, not videotape. The transmission of video images, via satellite, was still some years off. The distribution of the stories we covered depended upon the television networks. If you wanted to reach even a few hundred thousand people in one community, you needed access to the facilities of a local television station. No more.

We are on the verge of moving into the age of fibre optics. Once fibre optic cables are introduced into the majority of American homes, it will be a simple matter to send video images over the telephone. Anyone with a Hi-8 video camera and a laptop computer will have the technological wherewithal to become a "television network." Certainly, in its loosest definition, a television network is nothing more than an amalgam of consumers, around the country, capable of receiving the same material from a single provider. That definition can now be applied to any individual with a few thousand dollars and a desire to put video material on the Internet.

Consider the implications: the Internet, originally designed by the U.S. Defense establishment to be survivable, even in the event of nuclear war, can soon be "accessed" by millions of providers—each of whom is a mininetwork. If the provider chooses to remain anonymous, we can judge neither that person's reliability nor his agenda (or gender). The provider may be an isolated person or an organized group. To the extent that video images can be edited or altered, the consumer has nothing by which to gauge the value of the information that is being conveyed.

In such an environment, one would hope that Americans would turn in droves to the established journalists whose identities, backgrounds, and credentials they do know. In fact, however, journalists have rarely been held in lower regard. In what may be one of the more tragic convergences in American history, public trust in reporters has reached an all-time low at precisely the time that the country is about to be inundated in information chaos. And to make matters even worse, the chaos is being peddled as a form of electronic democracy.

America may not want to believe it, but it has never had a greater need for its professional press corps. Reporters and news organizations may not want to hear it, but the country has never had a greater need for serious, no-nonsense reporting.

We would like you to meet some old-fashioned reporters. Read their stories and hear their message. You'll miss them when they're gone.

— Ted Koppel

Preface

While there is a growing body of literature about the networks and the stars of the networks, the news anchors, there is relatively little attention paid to the working journalists—the network correspondents—who day after day are in the field gathering the news and who night after night deliver it to the American people in a form that tells their story coherently for the day's broadcast.

Southern Illinois University at Carbondale was in a position to remedy that by putting the spotlight on four of our distinguished graduates. At the initial suggestion of Dean Joe Foote, we decided to invite Jim Bittermann, Chris Bury, Roger O'Neil, and Walter Rodgers back to their alma mater for a weekend of reflection and dialogue on their careers, their professions, and the changes they had observed in the role of the network correspondent during the span of their professional lifetimes.

First and foremost, these are people who like to write and talk. It is what they do for a living, and they are good at it. The exchanges were open, friendly, and fun. The correspondents seemed to enjoy it, and the audience certainly sensed a special chemistry between the four participants. The correspondents were very forthcoming about their experiences during the conference. In fact, you may first want to read the chapter "Dialogue from the Trenches" before the rest of the book in order to put the whole situation into perspective.

These men are at the top of their profession as is evidenced by the fact that Bittermann anchored CNN's coverage from Paris of Princess Diana's tragic accident; Bury has covered presidential campaigns and major Clinton White House stories for *Nightline*; O'Neil was the lead reporter for NBC's coverage of the Oklahoma City bombing and the Timothy McVeigh trial; and Rodgers, as CNN bureau chief in Jerusalem, has covered numerous high profile bombings, retaliations, and peace discussions in the Middle East.

Because it is not possible in the course of a short conference to include all angles relating to a correspondent's job, we invited others in the field to contribute to this book. George Strait of ABC News discusses how race has played a significant role in his career. Marlene Sanders, formerly of ABC and CBS, describes what it was like to be a woman correspondent in the early years and how that role has evolved today. CNN's Garrick Utley explains the demise of the foreign correspondent on network news today from his perspective as a former international correspondent for ABC and NBC. Professor Michael Murrie discusses how technology affects correspondents' work. Ed Turner of CNN sets the stage for the correspondents' discussion of the "trenches."

These correspondents reflect in some depth on the role of the correspondent, how it was when they started, how it is now, and how it may be evolving. Their theme is that change is the only constant in their lives as the network news industry has developed and evolved over the past three decades. The changes are driven by the economics of the industry, the technological changes, and the people who come and go. The technology in particular has changed so rapidly that news-gathering feats that would have been inconceivable thirty years ago are now commonplace. This is a world driven by satellites, cell phones, minicameras, and the laptop computer. The economic and business changes are also profound. The movement toward corporate mergers, greater concentration of corporate power in fewer hands, and the expectation that the news divisions will be profit centers for the mostly entertainment-centered corporations that own them has meant that life is increasingly centered on New York (or Atlanta) and the news producers stationed there.

Given the demands, pressures, costs, and sacrifices, one might well ask why they stay with such a difficult and demanding profession for a lifetime. When one listens carefully to these correspondents, it becomes clear that they are all compelled by some common commitments, values, and beliefs. They deeply believe that it is important to bring the daily news to the American people. They think that if there is a story out there, and there always is another one, then that story ought to be told. These are the people who take the First Amendment seriously because they believe the admonition that a well-informed electorate is necessary for a mass democracy to work well. They hold passionate beliefs about the importance of a free press and free speech for a free people.

To be sure, reporters and news correspondents are infamous for being cynical, jaded, travel-worn, jet-lagged, and just plain weary much of the time. The rigors of the American presidential campaign trail or the dangers of a war zone in the current international hot spot both take a heavy toll. Nevertheless, these are deeply idealistic and intellectual people. They must have a keen sense of history and a broad knowledge of economics, politics, technology, science, and a host of other more esoteric subjects that give their stories content and context. They bring a vast wealth of their own considerable contacts, a lifetime of reading and study, an incredible record of travel, a knowledge of past leaders, and a range of experiences that most of us can only appreciate vicariously, to the task of telling this story in this way on this day.

Ultimately then, the news correspondents are teachers and historians. They teach us, the audience, what we need to know about their subject, and they make the public record the instant history of that day. Increasingly, scholars are turning to that instant electronic record to study the events that shape American and world history. Collections like the Vanderbilt University Television News Archives, for example, provide scholars with systematic data bases of the electronic record that can be studied and analyzed for many years to come. We think this book will contribute to that long-term scholarly analysis and quest.

— John S. Jackson III

Acknowledgments

Four network correspondents, all alumni of Southern Illinois University at Carbondale, laid the foundation for this project. Jim Bittermann, Chris Bury, Roger O'Neil, and Walter Rodgers came to Carbondale from three continents to talk about the role of the network correspondent, to write about their ideas, and to lend their support. These four highly respected correspondents, all at the top of their game, represent the very best of their profession, and we are proud to have them as alumni. We were indeed fortunate to have excellent supplementary contributions from George Strait, Marlene Sanders, Ed Turner, Garrick Utley, and Mike Murrie.

Second only to the correspondents' contributions in making this book possible are those of my colleague and friend, Provost John Jackson, who co-directed the conference and supported this effort throughout. John's masterful direction of the conference's first panel and his excellent advice on the shape of this book have been invaluable. Only modesty kept him from being a coeditor of this work.

Cindy Price, a Ph.D. student in journalism, has been exceptionally helpful in the preliminary editing of the manuscript and in attending to a myriad of details in getting it to press. The product of Cindy's fine work can be found throughout the book.

I would like to thank all those who made the correspondents' conference successful: the McCroy family through the Paul F. McCroy endowment, who funded the conference; CNN, WPSD-TV, and WSIL-TV who also provided financial support; and Marilyn Lingle who performed superbly in arranging the correspondents' conference with strong support from Tim Boudreau, Pansy Jones, Bob Hageman, Robert Henderson, and Jill Belcher.

The staff of Southern Illinois University Press has been extraordinarily supportive from the beginning.

Finally, thanks to the correspondents who have cooperated with academics and told their stories so that others might learn about their work.

Live from the Trenches

1
Introduction

Joe S. Foote

F ew occupational specialties have held as much fulfillment during the
second half of the twentieth century as the job of a network news
correspondent. When Edward R. Murrow's "boys" fanned out across
Europe before World War II, they enjoyed remarkable independence and
power. Murrow's correspondents had a pipeline directly into the living
rooms of the American people, and during the uncertainties of wartime,
the nation hung on every word. A country in search of heroes and celebrities added "broadcast correspondent" to its repertoire.

The positive image of the network correspondent soared during
the sixties when a slew of great stories took television news to center
stage. From moon landings to assassinations to the civil rights struggle
and the Vietnam War, television eclipsed newspapers as America's chief
source of information. The broadcast correspondent became a fixture of
American journalism as correspondents' prestige and access increased
with every major story.

It is the fascinating image of Murrow and his television succes-
sors—freewheeling, independent, globe-trotting journalists—that frames
the public portrait of a modern correspondent. The position of network
correspondent remains one of the most sought after positions in journalism. Yet, the job is not what it used to be. Today's sobering reality of cost
cutting and central control has sullied the idealized image of the network correspondent and has encouraged an angst that is overtaking the
correspondent corps.

Like all industries in the eighties, the business of broadcast news
changed, and with it the employees who worked there. Rocked to their
core by mergers and increased competition, the networks quickly whipped
themselves into profit centers. Correspondents suffered. Insecurity and
uncertainty overtook professionals who swaggered invincibly just two
decades earlier. Change sapped the correspondents' autonomy, security,
and loyalty to their news organizations.

There is no shortage of literature on the American television networks and their stars—the evening news anchors and prime time personalities. Network news has been dissected and inspected from every conceivable angle by academics, pundits, critics, and practitioners. Yet, the role of correspondents, the foot soldiers of network news, has been largely overlooked. Their story has been stuffed obscurely between the lines of the larger network story. This chapter is an overview and historical perspective for a book that is the first examination of network television news correspondents and their work, much of it coming from the correspondents themselves.

Ascension

With the positive and influential role model of the radio correspondent of World War II etched into recent memory, network executives plunged into the television age leading with their correspondent strength. Television correspondents were mostly the same journalists who made a name in radio, but few embraced the new medium in the beginning. It was left to young, second-string correspondents, like Douglas Edwards of CBS and David Brinkley of NBC, to charge voluntarily and energetically into television, leapfrogging some of the reluctant veterans. Eventually all came on board, and the television news age began.

Early television news was really radio news supplemented by a few pictures. Bulky cameras limited the correspondents' geographical range and made getting on the air a struggle. Deadlines were artificially early to meet the constraints of the medium. Using a format that still dominates the newscasts, correspondents dispatched to a news story did "stand-ups" at the scene, adding "B Roll" film later to amplify the story; only the advent of the "live shot" would enhance the model.

The early broadcast news format established the field correspondent as the primary gatherer and reporter of news, and the correspondent report as the content backbone. Anchors knitted together a disparate set of correspondent dispatches into a coherent product. Rarely did an anchor do an extended story, except during special events like a political convention or a space shot; the correspondents were undisputed creators of the content of network news.

The twenty-year period from 1960 to 1980 represented the correspondents' "glory days." Budgets were flush, network news was growing in stature and popularity, there were only three competitors to serve a huge domestic market, correspondents had significant independence, and they dominated the newscast. During this period of skyrocketing morale and upward mobility, the role of the correspondent solidified. New York controlled the evening news broadcast, but correspondents had considerable independence. Top correspondents held specific beats or geographical territories. The domestic prestige beats were all in Washington with the White House, Congress, and the State Department heading the list; overseas—London, Moscow, and the hot spot du jour topped the pecking order.

Upwardly mobile correspondents rotated through a variety of assignments, ending up at a prestige beat like the White House. When CBS and NBC expanded their broadcasts to 30 minutes in 1963, correspondents gained additional opportunities for exposure. During the next decade, high profile stories like the Vietnam War, the civil rights struggle, the space race, the cold war, and political assassinations provided a launching pad for a whole generation of correspondents. Talented young reporters rapidly climbed the television market ladder to the pinnacle of network news. Hundreds of others endured low pay and shaky job security in the hope that they one day would join the chosen network few.

Stories about obscure local reporters being "discovered" by the networks while covering a major spot news story became legion. At the top of network folklore was CBS's Dan Rather—being catapulted to the network after reporting from the eye of a hurricane in Texas, then soaring to the White House as the CBS Dallas-based correspondent when the Kennedy assassination story unfolded. Just enough unknowns ascended to keep the network dream alive. Having so many in the hunt for a coveted network correspondent's job only enhanced the prestige of those who had already made it to the top.

During the sixties, the correspondent corps became the breeding ground for anchorpersons when the networks elevated substantive journalists with years of reporting experience rather than relying on news readers in the British tradition. For correspondents, the anchor slot became the pinnacle position. Anchors promoted through this system, however, often became embarrassed by the small amount of heavy lifting required in their new positions and clung to the correspondent title as a badge of honor.

Demand for correspondents' work soared when big news stories unfolded. Not only was there the evening news—the network flagship broadcast—but morning news programs, news specials, and radio as well. Rather than flood the market with an army of correspondents, the networks empowered a trusted few with more responsibility and gave them better resources to do their work. Correspondents headed four-person crews that included a producer, cameraperson, and sound technician. Sometimes a lighting technician, assistant producer, and a unit manager came aboard. Thus, the correspondent became a network prince of sorts with his/her own retinue of courtiers to provide support.

Correspondents basked in their greatest glory during the mega-stories when money was no object, and New York would move heaven and earth to get them to the scene. It wasn't unusual on a big story to have a network "bag man" with a fist full of hundred dollar bills running interference for the network juggernaut. Pouring more and more money into the care and feeding of correspondents created a much-envied occupation and lifestyle. Chartering jets at will became the status symbol of the newly empowered correspondents, with a variety of secondary perks following closely behind.

Not only did network correspondents have the biggest budgets, but their stock as journalists was rising as well. Print reporters who used to turn up their noses at their lower status broadcast colleagues found themselves being gradually, but undeniably, pushed to the rear of the gallery. Public officials and high profile news sources eagerly sought the network correspondents first because they could deliver their views to an enormous nationwide audience. Unlike their European counterparts that were national in scope, American newspapers were inherently local and could less and less frequently make a national splash. Neither could newspaper reporters project the force of their personality as well as television reporters.

Competition

Overspending was never a sin during the go-go days of network news, but getting beaten on a story was. As long as correspondents remained productive and competitively agile, the power and wealth of the news division was there to support them anywhere in the world. The television networks engaged in hand-to-hand combat 365 days a year with each side keeping score. Competition became an obsession. "Victories" often were measured in seconds, even though a network scoop that caused the adrenaline to pump at network centers in New York was often insignificant to viewers.

Producers kept score on correspondents as if the public were intensely viewing all three networks simultaneously, the way Lyndon Johnson did in the White House. Extended postmortem sessions in New York followed every newscast. Producers weren't shy about making frank comparisons among correspondents and assigning blame. Woe to the correspondent who didn't measure up. As former CBS President Frank Stanton once said about the inter-network competition, the veins tightening in his neck, "I wouldn't want to be second, and I damn sure wouldn't want to be third" (1985).

At first, the competition was limited to CBS and NBC, but underfunded ABC caught up and eventually passed its elder brothers in the eighties. The correspondents were the infantrymen whom the field marshals in New York sent into daily battle. From the war room in New York, the producers moved pieces on the board in anticipation of the competition's next move. News executives scrutinized correspondent productivity closely. With fewer than 10 correspondents appearing daily on each of three newscasts before the largest television audience in the world, there was no place to hide.

The stakes were so high that competition for competition's sake frequently reigned. Correspondents were not always used productively to gather stories, but to "stake out" locations where a news maker might make a pronouncement deemed an exclusive. The networks assigned a correspondent 24 hours a day to the president, just in case there was an assassination attempt. Rather than take pool footage of routine video, the networks insisted on being there themselves, often with a correspondent. Much of this individuality was purely cosmetic because, in the aggregate, the network broadcasts were becoming remarkably similar with at least two of the networks leading with the same story 90 percent of the time. At least two-thirds of the content during the seventies was nearly identical (Foote and Steele 1986).

The Beat

Television news took its cue from newspapers and followed a modified beat system to track and report news. Yet, unlike newspapers, the networks sought only 22 minutes of content from a half dozen correspondents each day and could not afford to station correspondents permanently in too many venues. Most of the networks' beats were in Washington— White House, State Department, Capitol Hill, Pentagon, Supreme Court—where the weekly yield of reports could justify the expenditure of keeping a correspondent there. More than half of the network news output came from Washington, where a majority of the correspondents were stationed. As serious news organization wanna-bes, the networks were obliged to have permanent correspondents at the prestige beats in Washington where correspondents would be hand-fed a daily diet of government news.

The network nerve center in New York housed the second largest stable of correspondents. Bureaus located in Chicago, Los Angeles, and wherever the networks owned affiliates were also prominent. Other geographic areas fared far less well. Studies showed a distorted coverage map with some major cities and states getting disproportionate coverage and some receiving no coverage at all.

Anyone viewing network news in its early days could clearly see the Washington/East Coast axis at work. The networks could assemble a respectable evening newscast without ever leaving Washington and New York. Much of the coverage was tied to institutional settings like the White House, the Capitol, and the State Department. A three-hour time difference discriminated against West Coast stories. Cost kept out-of-the-way places from breaking into the news flow except during periods of crisis.

Trying to keep their image from the Murrow days, the networks maintained bureaus in European capitals where they had been so successful before—London, Rome, Paris, Berlin. Eventually, the networks dispatched correspondents to Cairo, Johannesburg, Tokyo, and Moscow. The stationing of correspondents during the glory days of television news reflected a decidedly Eurocentric view of the world. London, Paris, and Rome seemed far more important than Delhi, Lagos, or Bangkok where no correspondent was placed.

Initially, the networks tried to launch bureaus in obscure places, but the payoff was never realized. PBS anchor Robert MacNeil recalled being dispatched as a young NBC correspondent to the Congo where he dutifully filed reports that New York routinely ignored (MacNeil, 1982). Except for perennial hot spots like the Middle East, there were hardly any permanent correspondents assigned to developing countries. The Latin American correspondents were typically headquartered in Miami where direct air service to South America was the best. Horror stories abounded about correspondents making multiple connections on airlines no one had heard of to get to a story that was never aired on the evening news.

The typical correspondent life cycle featured multiple moves from one assignment to the next along a generally upward mobility path from general assignment reporter to regional correspondent to beat or foreign correspondent and perhaps to anchor. Like in any corporation, however, not making the usual climb up the ladder can be hazardous to a career unless the organization sees particular value in geographic stability. It was possible, however, for correspondents with a particular aptitude or geographical preference to spend most of their careers on a particular assignment. Roger O'Neil in Denver and Jim Bittermann in Europe are good examples; each have been on the same basic beat for nearly two decades because of the niches they have carved through their own expertise and enterprise.

At first, all correspondents were generalist reporters, but specialists became popular in the seventies when medical, legal, and science correspondents emerged. The career paths of specialist correspondents were a radical departure from the norm of reporters working their way up the affiliate ladder to the networks. Many of the specialists had no previous broadcasting experience; they came directly from their professions to the networks. Seeing persons transformed instantly into network-level correspondents must have grated on some of those who had paid their dues on the traditional rocky road to the network pinnacle.

Specialist reporters proved that making the transition to network news was neither easy nor impossible. There were abundant horror stories of abysmal failure; some quit voluntarily after only a few goes. Yet there were clearly success stories, especially with those who had already proven themselves as highly regarded print journalists. Once the TV experience barrier had been broken, several newspaper reporters gravitated to network news. Later came a motley group from other professions—lawyers, doctors, judges, generals. By the time retired General Norman Schwarzkopf began doing a feature for NBC in the mid-nineties, network executives seemed open to anyone who could increase ratings and bring pizzazz to the broadcast without significantly affecting journalistic quality.

The Great Divide

The first half century of network television news can be divided roughly into two eras: the loss-leader years 1950–1980 and the profit center years 1981–1999. During the formative years, network news was always a costly, but necessary item in the network budget. Networks built their franchises and credibility in Washington on the reputations of news organizations that hemorrhaged revenue. A mark of honor was to sacrifice the prime time schedule and its handsome revenue to cover a presidential speech, political convention, or breaking news story.

Yet this "unscheduled news" caused expanding fault lines behind the scenes between the news division that promoted the broadcasts and the entertainment division that sacrificed prime-time revenue because of them. The correspondents and anchors loved grabbing prime time from the entertainment divisions because it meant huge audiences and more airtime than they could ever get on the evening news. The "suits" in the executive suites cringed every time the news people came calling.

Ironically, it was during these money-losing days for network news that the correspondents enjoyed their greatest independence, highest morale, most lavish lifestyle, and widest budgetary latitude. Correspondents had as much money as they needed when news was a loss leader. It was when news finally became a profit center that management tightened the financial screws on the correspondents.

CBS's *60 Minutes* was the networks' first news cash cow and their first regular venture into prime time. Being positioned on the fringe of prime time after professional football on Sunday, the biggest viewing night of the year, large audiences automatically meant big money. The *60 Minutes* experience led to the production of other magazine-style programs in the evening that competed head-on with entertainment programming. Executives quickly realized that there was far more money to be made in prime time than with the evening news; yet, even the flagship broadcasts became profitable eventually.

When the prime time money machine began churning, the entire dynamic of the network news system changed. The insulation between news and entertainment eroded as the bottom line applied equally to news as entertainment. The evening news broadcasts remained partially sheltered, but the news divisions became big time profit centers with a prime time fixation. In some cases, news became more profitable than entertainment. Even news programs that finished last made money because their production costs were so low. The skyrocketing cost of talent and production for prime time entertainment shows pushed forward a rush of inexpensive news and reality-based programs.

The profitability of prime time news programming gave the beleaguered news divisions a reprieve from their downward spiral, but the field correspondents did not share in the riches. The magazine shows were producer-driven rather than correspondent-driven. Using the *60 Minutes* model, segment producers did all of the research and preliminary interviews, waiting until the end of the story to summon the correspondent. It could take as few as three correspondents to front for an entire hour of programming. Prime time magazines also had a habit of stealing story ideas from the evening news correspondents to use for longer magazine segments. Programs replaced news beats as the measuring stick of network news spending.

The emergence of prime time magazine correspondents planted a new tier of talent between the anchors and the journeyman correspondents. The prime time correspondents were better paid, had higher prestige, and reached far more viewers than their evening news counterparts. Field correspondents, thus, had to settle for third-tier status in this new hierarchy.

Despite a profitable move into prime time, the network news divisions faced serious challenges. New ownership of the networks, a declining audience share, new competition from cable, and the rising power of local news caused major change. The presumed cure for the network ills was downsizing. Management consultants swooped into the newsrooms in the mid-eighties with questions. Why was it so expensive to gather the news? Why did correspondents get on the air so little but cost so much? Why did it take so many staff and resources to support the correspondent? Would it not be cheaper to buy-in coverage from a reliable, third-party source rather than always send a network's own correspondent to cover an event? Should not correspondents be reporting for more news programs to make their positions more cost effective?

During this period of management consultant influence, correspondents and bureaus started to disappear. CBS President Lawrence Tisch finished an international tour of the news division in the mid-eighties by decrying opulence and overstaffing in the overseas bureaus. Tisch and the management consultants never grasped the principle of redundancy necessary to staff a bureau's second day coverage with reinforcements. What they had would be good enough, they reasoned, considering the immense savings gained from lowering the news-gathering overhead. CBS and NBC whittled their forces to levels unbelievable for those who had dominated the globe just a decade before. By 1998, the networks had but a handful of foreign correspondents to cover the world. Global coverage was a Potemkin facade the networks constructed to hide the shell of a correspondent corps left behind.

A dramatic example of the networks' empty stable of correspondents occurred on August 31, 1997, in Paris, France, when Princess Diana died. Neither ABC, CBS, nor NBC had a correspondent stationed permanently in Paris. All three had permanent reporters there a decade earlier. CNN's Jim Bittermann, operating from Paris for more than 15 years and speaking fluent French, was the only broadcast reporter who seemed to know the lay of the land. The *American Journalism Review* reported:

> Satellite vans clogged the tiny side streets, transforming the historic Ile de la Cite into a Felliniesque media carnival. At one point, when a lawyer for one of the accused photographers emerged, the anxious crowd surged forward, ready to uplink the latest crumb of information. "Can you give us a few quotes?" a desperate correspondent called out—not to the lawyer but to CNN's bilingual contributing correspondent, Paris veteran Jim Bittermann. "It's just depressing," Bittermann remarked later, referring to the latest big media trend: closing overseas bureaus and drop-shipping clueless roving reporters during times of need. (Durocher 1997, 10)

With fewer correspondents in the field to gather news, parachute journalism became the norm for nearly all international correspondents and some domestic ones. Being based in London did not mean just cruising the Whitehall and Westminster for stories, but being prepared to circulate in a 1,000 mile radius from home on a moment's notice. In this environment, knowing the local language or being intimate with the culture gave way to having street smarts and an incredible ability to assimilate and process information under highly stressful conditions.

Fortunately, the networks had a highly talented corps of veteran correspondents with years of international experience who could fly to the scene and usually get the story right with very little preparation. Yet, the practice was a perilous one that increased the possibility of error and kept the correspondents from building the background and source contacts to do their very best.

Networks frequently operated under the illusion that they could actually cover the world with a skeleton crew of correspondents and were all too willing to send reporters into unknown territory poorly equipped to cover the story. To combat this inherent disadvantage, correspondents developed shortcuts to information and sources to keep from being totally embarrassed until they could get their bearings. Sometimes correspondents relied on little more than notes from a producer and a quick call to Western diplomats before going on the air. The good correspondents managed to land on their feet with a highly credible report, but too often the flaws of parachute journalism were apparent.

Domestically, the networks began relying more on local affiliates for news. In the glory days, the networks would do anything to get their own person to the scene and politely declined most affiliate offers of help. But the leaner networks were quite happy to rely on an affiliate reporter. With the major local markets sporting television news talent comparable to the networks, the fall off in quality was much less apparent than the veteran correspondents were willing to admit.

During the late seventies and early eighties, the affiliates in major markets moved boldly ahead, brandishing high dollar budgets, anchors of near-network quality, and greatly expanded news-gathering ability. Ambitious affiliates used their satellite trucks to compete head-on with the networks on national stories and even ventured overseas to get a local angle on international news. To hold off the affiliates from becoming direct competitors, the networks geared-up news services exclusively to feed local stations. Unlike earlier times when affiliates got only the leftovers from the network table, they now received a piping hot main course; correspondent reports began appearing on local stations even before they aired on the evening news.

The networks faced competition on a second major front when the Cable News Network appeared in 1980 with 24 hours of continuous news. Nicknamed the "Chicken Noodle Network" by its derisive network colleagues, CNN was a pale imitation of the venerable network giants—manned by local affiliate wanna-bes, recent j-school graduates, and network retreads. Yet it had something the other networks could only dream of—a 24-hour news hole. CNN news executive Ed Turner always called ABC, CBS, and NBC the "entertainment networks," careful to draw a clear distinction between those that ventured into news part-time and those that were dedicated solely to the practice of journalism.

CNN opened the gates of opportunity for a new generation of correspondents but set a budget far below the standard to which network correspondents had become accustomed. Smaller crews, Spartan travel allowances, and meager perquisites dominated. At a time when the new owners of the big three were eagerly looking for ways to cut costs, CNN provided them with a working prototype of how cheaply news could be gathered.

Within three years, CNN was no joke but was a full-fledged competitor. By nature, CNN was a correspondent's network. Extensive news gathering and on-the-spot reporting of breaking news became CNN's calling card. CNN downplayed the role of anchors, allowing the correspondents to shine. Nowhere to be seen at CNN were the strangling time constraints, the producer meddling, and the lack of airtime. CNN correspondents' only problems were frantically trying to feed the beast and maintain a reasonable level of professionalism.

Live shots and constant demand for reports seasoned green correspondents far before their time. CNN outshined its network competition during the Gulf War partly because its correspondent corps had so many more repetitions than some of the weekday warriors of ABC, CBS, and NBC. CNN showed that doing more news than your competition could enhance correspondent performance. However, going live sometimes made work difficult for CNN correspondents because they did not have time to "report" the story.

Correspondents could be tethered to the camera for hours, relying on assistants to gather information and repeating what producers were feeding them in their earpiece with no firsthand sense of what was happening. This was especially frustrating when correspondents had to go on the air immediately after arriving on the scene of a story. The imperative to go live affected the other networks as well. ABC's Ted Koppel explained how this technology drives the story.

> (The reporter) is bound to the transmission point, while producers and camera crews go out and gather material. Frequently, since the producers and videotape editors have to put together the packages that will air on the various programs, only the camera crews are available to actually go out and gather material. They, for obvious reasons, are more concerned with the visual; so, despite the fact that more people than ever before are in the field disseminating news, there is less time and less focus than ever before on the actual gathering of editorial material. (1994, 16)

Flanked by the twin competition from CNN and local news, ABC, CBS, and NBC were forced to redefine their news product. Assuming that viewers would have already watched news of the big stories before the evening news was broadcast, the networks opted for more reflection, stylized reporting, longer trend stories, and a hint of "infotainment." What they lacked in immediacy and news-gathering ability around the world, the networks tried to make up for with a well-regarded brand name, trusted anchors, and a highly talented, experienced correspondent corps.

Producer-Driven Networks

Changes in the network news format gave producers an opportunity to tighten the command and control structure of the evening news broadcast. Network news would no longer be just a composite of the latest news of the day cobbled together with breakneck speed. It would be a selective portrait of the world carefully crafted by the executive producer and staff on a tighter budget. Producers had always scrutinized stories carefully, but deadlines and a culture of correspondent autonomy had held their power in check. As budgets tightened, the power of the managing producers increased.

Stringent budgets meant fewer stories commissioned. Gone were the days when correspondents did a spate of stories on spec and eventually got a few of them on the air. Correspondents began covering more of what producers wanted and fewer stories the correspondents initiated. The truly international story with no immediate and compelling American angle, never a popular item in New York, became a casualty of the news-gathering process. Only CNN had the airtime luxury to thrive in this area. Doing fewer stories meant less work for ABC, CBS, and NBC correspondents covering remote areas that rarely made the news, putting their jobs and bureaus in jeopardy.

The producers who commissioned a story often prescribed the content. Correspondents chafed at the numerous, often contradictory, rewrites demanded by producers. Every network correspondent has war stories about how the butchers in New York decimated a story. Correspondents lament that by the time "stories by committee" are broadcast, their creative imprint has vanished. Executive producers have their own preferences for types of stories and presentation styles that frequently override correspondent initiative.

Network correspondents who have fled to CNN marvel at their new-found independence. Enterprise stories nearly always find airtime, and the editing process is much less severe. Most editing occurs at the bureau rather than Atlanta. To insure quality, bureau chiefs often have to impose a higher editing standard on themselves than headquarters producers require.

As budgetary pressures grew, more and more stories appeared on the evening news that were assembled by correspondents but not actually reported by them. Producers asked New York and Washington correspondents to do stories from the bureau that happened somewhere else. Without ever visiting the scene of the story, correspondents would try to report authoritatively on a story they never actually covered, relying on footage from a variety of locations. It really was, in Edward Epstein's words, "News from Nowhere."

Another variation on this theme was for the White House correspondent to give a presidential angle to an out-of-Washington story. For example, the death of a foreign leader could be reported from the White House or State Department rather than from the target country. While this tactic offered great economy to the networks, it took a huge step backward in the standards of field reporting. It also frequently distorted the reality of the story by giving the White House angle disproportionate influence. Under this network logic, almost any domestic or international story could be reported from Washington.

Taking a cue from their infotainment cousins, some long-form stories on the evening news began having an edge placed on them—an unambiguous perspective that drove home the overriding message in the story in a one-dimensional way. This heavy-handed scripting of the story greatly eroded the autonomy of the correspondent. Roger O'Neil in his chapter describes how correspondents assigned to do a "Fleecing of America" segment on NBC are put in a story-angle straitjacket that robs them of their own perspective and distorts reality. When the story comes preordained from New York, the correspondent is asked to assemble the pieces together in the assigned order but not to rearrange the content. This fundamentally negates the role of the correspondent as a primary gatherer and interpreter of information.

The tightening of story control by New York greatly depressed correspondent morale. At the same time that correspondents saw their ranks decline, their lifestyle erode, and their workload expand, their birthright of independence came under assault from within. Over the years, New York has won an increasingly high percentage of the correspondent/producer battles. Frequently, correspondents are left sulking in the field, questioning their role in the network news-gathering system. When correspondents were more autonomous, being 5,000 miles away from the home base was an advantage. But when the locus of power shifted to headquarters, an outpost mentality prevailed. Isolated, correspondents began second-guessing their status in the hierarchy and their role in the network news-gathering system.

The belief that unwritten "A" and "B" lists of in-favor and out-of-favor correspondents governed who got on the news stoked the growing insecurity of the correspondent corps. Was the person reporting the story becoming more important than the story itself, and what were the crite-

ria for making the "A" list and staying there? How far could a correspondent go in arguing with producers? There were just enough cases
where anchors or producers had barred a correspondent from the evening
news to keep the "A-B list" paranoia alive. There is hardly a correspondent who has not at one time felt a deep insecurity after hanging up the
phone with New York, worried about being blacklisted.

Simmering below the surface of the executive producer/correspon-
dent relationship is a resentment of the power producers wield and how
they attained it. What particularly grates on the correspondents is that
the executive producers of the evening news come from the producer
corps, a group that the correspondents have always directed as subordi-
nates. It is like drawing the generals from the enlisted ranks with
the majors and captains caught in the middle. While rarely discussed
openly, correspondent resentment of the topsy-turvy chain of comm-
and could be blamed for a variety of organizational ills in the network
news system.

The Big Foot

The New York producers, while powerful, still faced competition for
control of the broadcast from the evening news anchors who fancied
themselves as majordomos of the broadcast. Anchors have diluted producers' power by ensconcing themselves in the position of "managing
editor," a phantom position awkwardly squeezed into the network hierarchy to appease the autonomous anchors. Rather than act as a
counterbalance to the producers on behalf of the correspondents, the
anchors have made the situation worse for their former colleagues. The
correspondent-turned-anchors can be just as brutal and judgmental as
the producers. With the managing editor title tacked onto their duties,
anchors have banished several correspondents into oblivion, leaving little
recourse for appeal.

Anchors can not only influence how often correspondents' stories
are chosen for air but can also steal the stories out from under the correspondents. Anchors' natural instincts are to rush to the field to do
high-profile stories, temporarily displacing a correspondent. Few things
provoke correspondents like being "big-footed" by an anchor. Correspondents get the double whammy not only because they are upstaged
by a higher-status person but also because they lose the chance to cover
the very best and most visible stories on their beats.

When anchors began making mega-salaries and became signature
players, the pressure to put anchors on the air only increased, denying
good stories to correspondents. As Penn Kimball wrote, "Television news
has a lot more to do with the presenter than the material being presented" (Kimball 1994, 4). Producers found that it was much cheaper

and more efficient to have anchors read stories from the anchor desk with taped inserts than to rely on a correspondent report from the field.

The reliance on anchors over correspondents is more than cosmetic. It shifts the center of gravity from news gathering to news processing. When a correspondent reports a story, there is considerable news gathering in the field. A studio-based story using an anchor, however, presents the same story using hired-in footage from news wholesalers. An astute viewer of television news notices the anchor doing more and more stories from the studio amplified by video taken at the scene, but with no correspondent. Most of the time, anchor-based stories are a matter of necessity or cost because no network correspondent has been assigned to the story. Sometimes, however, anchors report from the studio when a correspondent is already on the scene ready and willing to report. This behavior clearly hits a raw nerve in any correspondent caught short by the intervening anchor.

Getting on the Air

In a competitive, bottom-line environment where jobs and livelihoods are at stake, correspondents must be visible frequently on the high profile news programs. Not getting on the air is an ongoing worry of correspondents. Only the senior reporter at the White House can count on getting almost daily access to the evening news; everyone else has to wait their turn.

During the 15 years that I have kept statistics on correspondent visibility, the majority of correspondents get on the air less than once a week; only the top 10 will do more than two reports per week. The average number of reports per correspondent on the evening news in 1997 was 37 compared to 43 in 1993. Below the most visible 100 correspondents, reporters rarely get on the air more than every other week. As anchors do more and more of the work correspondents used to do, the number of correspondent reports per broadcast is steadily decreasing.

In 1984, there were 234 correspondents reporting regularly for the evening news at all three networks. Today, there are only 167—a decrease of nearly 30 percent. The number of correspondents reporting for the evening news has declined by nearly 20 percent in just five years as downsizing has taken its toll. The geographic spread of existing correspondents is also different as bureaus have been downgraded and closed. Bureaus like Chicago, which might have had three or four correspondents a decade ago, are now lucky to have one.

Assignment has always played a significant role in a correspondent's visibility. The beat reporters in Washington and some specialist reporters are almost guaranteed regular exposure on the evening news. Of all the correspondents who have been ranked among the most visible during the past fifteen years, 80 percent have had Washington assignments. Regional and foreign correspondents are much more dependent on the news flow. Reporters in the Los Angeles bureau during the O. J. Simpson trial or in the Middle East during the Gulf War gained intense levels of visibility during those particular stories. Yet, there can be equally long periods of drought. When one particular area is hot, coverage opportunities automatically shrink for the remaining correspondents. If 10 minutes per night is taken by the "big story," little airtime is left for everyone else.

Correspondents can increase their exposure by volunteering for breaking news or special assignments. Being in a high-profile war zone has proven to be a reliable visibility enhancer for any correspondent. On the domestic side, Robert Hager of NBC has become one of the most visible network correspondents by being on-call 24 hours a day to tackle the big stories wherever they occur. In the years 1987 and 1996, Hager appeared on the evening news more than any other correspondent, including those covering the White House; he is the only correspondent to have been on the list of the 10 most visible correspondents each of the last fifteen years. Producers know that Hager will leave on a moment's notice to cover a story anywhere in the world and will always turn in a solid performance. Hager's visibility has also been enhanced because he mines his regular beat of federal agencies in Washington better than any of his competitors.

Because the network assignment system creates automatic winners and losers, correspondents are sensitive to how assignment decisions are made. Minorities and women have long felt that the system discriminated against them. A disproportionate amount of the lower visibility general assignment positions have historically gone to women and minorities. During the eighties, women had virtually no upward mobility in the correspondent corps despite great gains being made nationally by women in other professions. It wasn't until 1991 that women showed a significant move upward into the top echelon of correspondents, including White House assignments. The best year for women was 1994 when reported a quarter of all stories. That year, 3 of the 10 most visible correspondents were women. Three years later, women were reporting only 22 percent of the stories and had no correspondent in the top 10.

Minorities lagged behind women in their upward mobility at network news broadcasts, showing no appreciable progress until 1994 when they reported 13 percent of all stories on the evening news and had 17 of the top 100 correspondents. In 1997, 18 percent of correspondents were minorities and reported 15 percent of the stories. The ethnic breakdown of correspondents was 20 African-American, 5 Asian, and 3 Hispanic. In 15 years, there have been only 2 years where a minority reporter has finished among the top 10 most visible correspondents and that was because of extraordinary coverage of the O. J. Simpson trial and floods in the Midwest. Only a handful of African-American reporters have had a regular beat in network news, and because of high turnover, few have attained the seniority to claim a prestige beat.

When women and minorities finally started to achieve upward mobility, layoffs as well as early retirements at the end of the eighties took a disproportionate toll on white men. The number of white male correspondents has plummeted more than 45 percent in just 12 years. In the early eighties, white men held more than 80 percent of the correspondent jobs. That has slipped to 59 percent today.

CBS historically was the network most hospitable to women and minorities. At one point, nearly one-third of all CBS correspondent reports came from women and 22 percent from minorities. CBS sometimes had fewer women and minority correspondents but managed to get maximum productivity and visibility from them. Most recently, ABC has taken leadership from CBS. In 1997, 37 percent of ABC correspondents were women reporting 31 percent of the stories. NBC had lagged behind badly in the visibility of minorities but has quadrupled the number of minority reports from 4 to 16 percent of all stories during the past five years.

Lifestyle

The lifestyle of the network television news correspondent has always had its highs and lows: glamour, excitement, celebrity, financial security, and the rush of being in the middle of it all, contrasted with chronic professional insecurity and a stressful, fatiguing lifestyle that robs one of family time. Correspondents have never been able to reconcile the extremes of their profession, but the recent depression of morale causes them to think more about the negatives.

The falling by the wayside of so many of their colleagues has caused correspondents to take more than a passing glance at their own security, happiness, and well-being. Some have left the networks voluntarily after evaluating their own situation. Those who remain are constantly looking over their shoulder.

Regardless of whether correspondent morale is generally up or down, a clear negative attribute of the job is the toll taken by travel. Most correspondents spend a disproportionate amount of time struggling to get to where the news is being made. With fewer correspondents in the field, the distances between stories are magnified. Just the sheer amount of travel and time spent away from home causes hardship. For international correspondents, the travel may be across seven or eight time zones and radically different climates.

When a correspondent reaches the site of the story, the deadline clock begins ticking, requiring an indefatigable quality to persevere. The technology has accelerated the stress of the situation, forcing correspondents to report live from the scene minutes after they arrive. Feeding reports for multiple broadcasts puts the correspondent on an exhaustive treadmill until the next news cycle begins. For 24-hour networks like CNN, the day never ends.

A by-product of the killer travel schedules is less time spent with family. Among correspondents, divorce and neglect of children are legion. Yet, having a family, no matter how badly it is ignored, may be the correspondent's best pathway to a well-balanced life. Family acts as a constant counterweight to the total, single-minded dedication the job requires. Correspondents with nothing to go home to are the most vulnerable to professional myopia. "Boys on the bus" stories abound about how correspondents lose their perspective, becoming encapsulated in the world of a news story and drawing on this artificial environment for all of their daily emotional needs.

There appears to be a generational and gender divide concerning time for family. For years, network correspondents automatically pushed personal concerns aside to get to the story. It would have been unthinkable 20 years ago to decline an assignment because of a family conflict. A younger generation of correspondents, and especially women, are not as eager to travel at all costs on behalf of the network. They are trying much harder to balance their personal and professional lives. This requires a carefully orchestrated lifestyle that pushes as hard to find family time as it does to meet the excruciating demands of professional life.

Correspondents have found ways to rationalize some of the negatives of their lifestyles and to squeeze out as much family time as possible, but the risk of personal danger has been much more difficult to confront. Being sent to war zones and sites of regional conflict ups the ante for correspondents significantly. Some have already let it be known that, having dodged the bullet successfully for many years, they are not willing to take those kinds of risky assignments anymore, regardless of the setbacks to their career. Because so much airtime is routinely given to conflict, declining war assignments greatly lowers the odds of getting on the air. Conversely, those who are willing to tackle a dangerous assignment head-on can catapult their careers to stardom. More than one eager correspondent has made a name going where few wanted to go.

Celebrity has recently become a by-product of the correspondent's lifestyle. In a culture that places a premium on media exposure, it is no surprise that men and women who are seen by millions daily have a public persona. Visibility opens doors to opportunity, including books, lectures, talk show appearances, and so forth. Nearly all correspondents now have agents who negotiate their contracts with the networks and sometimes help in their "merchandising." Many correspondents will not make a public appearance, even on a college campus, without a sizable speaking fee.

There has been controversy recently over correspondents taking speaking fees from or having a financial stake in companies they cover. Clearly, journalists are no longer completely detached observers but are high profile, wealthy individuals whose private lives become entangled in their professional lives. Correspondents worried little about these problems years ago, but six and seven figure contracts have catapulted broadcast journalists into different tax brackets and social environments. It is not unusual for correspondents to socialize freely with politicians and other sources and to send their children to the same private schools. Critics argue that this improved lifestyle not only places correspondents too close to sources but puts the correspondent out of touch with most ordinary Americans.

Conclusion

Corporate downsizing, centralized administrative control, and resource cutbacks have dulled the correspondent's luster. Most alarming, news gathering has taken a back seat to news processing at most networks, marginalizing the role of the field correspondent. A 24-hour news network can exist today with no news-gathering capability whatsoever. In one all-news channel, recent j-school graduates packaged news from third-party sources around the clock with no correspondents and no original news gathering. Even major networks are camouflaging their shell of a correspondent corps by the clever use of anchors and third-party vendors.

Yet, there are limited signs of renewal in some sectors. At CNN, BBC, and other global networks, news gathering is on the increase with new bureaus opening where there was none before. NBC's and CBS's burgeoning cable efforts are setting the stage for a renewed interest in news gathering. News wholesalers are methodically fanning the globe to keep primary news gathering alive, although it leaves only two or three crews interpreting events for an entire world in some remote areas. Cyberjournalism offers a nascent, but promising, supplement to print and broadcast reporting.

There remains a bedrock belief in American journalism that gathering quality information is a prerequisite to quality journalism.

Correspondents, while diminished in role and stature, still form the backbone of the network news organizations. Some of the best journalism in the world is done by these senior journalists when they are given the freedom and resources to do their work. Changing roles are inevitable, but there will always be a need for good storytellers who can tell those stories concisely and articulately from firsthand experience.

Viewers should learn to discriminate between news organizations that gather their own news from the field and those that don't, and they should seek out news services that invest in people who report the news from where it is being made. The networks must realize what an incredibly valuable resource they have in their correspondent corps. It is this vast reserve of knowledge, talent, and experience that distinguishes network news organizations from their imitators and gives them vitality, insight, perspective, and credibility.

The time has come for news gathering, embodied by the quality of correspondents and their work, to retake center stage in the television news system. The challenge for the networks is to salvage a precious resource they have badly taken for granted.

References

Durocher, Debra D. 1997. Free press: "The front page" on speed. *American Journalism Review* (October): 10–11.

Epstein, Edward. 1973. *News from nowhere.* New York: Vintage Books.

Foote, Joe S. 1992. Women correspondents' visibility on the network evening news. *Mass Communications Review* 19: 36–40.

Foote, Joe S., and Michael E. Steele. 1986. Degree of conformity in lead stories in early evening network TV newscasts. *Journalism Quarterly* 63 (spring): 19–23.

Kimball, Penn. 1994. *Downsizing the news: Network cutbacks in the nation's capital.* Washington, D.C.: Woodrow Wilson CenterPress.

Koppel, Ted. 1994. Going live. *Communicator* (June): 16–18.

Lont, Cynthia M. 1995. *Women and the media: Content/careers/ criticism.* Belmont, CA: Wadsworth Publishing.

MacNeil, Robert. 1982. *The right place at the right time.* Boston: Little, Brown & Company.

Stanton, Frank (former president, CBS). 1985. Interview by author. New York, 24 January.

2
Bottom Feeders

Roger O'Neil

The formula is simple: Who, What, When, Where, Why, and How. It's the execution that's difficult. Six words to learn. Six words to practice. Six words never to be forgotten. Six words a profession called journalism has lived by.

So why do many people think of us as "bottom feeders"? You know, fish who scavenge the bottom of our tropical fish tanks scouring for scraps of food, dirty scraps none of the other fish want. Bottom feeders! That's what several people in Denver said recently when they were asked what they thought of news reporters. The survey said we were less trustworthy than used-car salesmen. On the list of least admired, we were lumped together with politicians. God! What happened? Who, What, When, Where, Why, and How?

The nightly news shows of network television are in a frenzy to label the news. On NBC, the network I am most familiar with since I have worked for the peacock for 17 years now, the joke is, "If it doesn't have a label, it doesn't get on the air!" It is not true, of course, but it's closer to the truth than I wish. We have "In Depth" part A and "In Depth" part B every night. There's "Health Watch" every Monday, unless a medical story pops up on Tuesday, Wednesday, Thursday, or Friday, in which case it can be called "Health Watch," too. "The Fleecing of America," a Wednesday feature, is a relatively new label that has met with overwhelming viewer approval or overwhelming viewer disgust depending on whose ox has been fleeced. More on fleecing later. Then there's "On Line," a so-called look beyond the headlines. I think that means news that's not important enough to warrant a story or stand on its own as a reader or voice-over; news that can, with the help of a computer-generated graphic behind the anchorman's shoulder, be lumped together into a quick series of one-liners. "On Line" is every night, except when there's not enough on-line to go on-line. "American Close-Up" is what it says it is, a Friday feature of an American who is doing something important enough to make a difference. NBC's most recent label is

"General Norman Schwarzkopf's American Hero." It is, as Broadway is fond of saying, a smash hit! Viewers have been complaining of gutter news so long that when a good news segment appeared on the network as local stations have been doing for many years, well that was news. Unfortunately, none of these reasons is why so much of the network nightly newscasts are now labeled.

Not so very long ago, the networks controlled the viewing audience from sign-on to sign-off. Then CNN came along—that outfit with Ted Turner, a rich kid who would go away when the money ran out, or so conventional wisdom thought. The networks didn't worry about Ted's kids. They were children in a man's game. Then Ted's kids slowly, but surely, became the network we all watched when we were on the road traveling. If you wanted to know what was happening in the world, you'd watch CNN. It wasn't good, but it did inform. Today it is good, and it still informs. CNN still doesn't have a lot of viewers (news correspondents for the other networks don't count), but there are enough that Mr. Turner has become something of a hornet. Push the clock ahead to 1996, and NBC teamed up with Microsoft to launch its own version of CNN. ABC offered the executive producer of *NBC Nightly News* a fat salary to jump ship and start its version of CNN. CBS is doing the same thing, although at least one executive there seemed to be thinking clearly when he suggested the all-news cable field may be getting a bit crowded. Before the rush to create Ted Turner look-alikes, a whole bunch of other networks sprouted. The most notable is FOX, but there are religious, sports, cooking, business, and numerous other networks on the air now with no end in sight. Those other networks considerably broaden the definition of the word "network" as we've come to think of it. In the years ahead, with hundreds of new cable channels and the ability of viewers to tune those signals in, another definition of what a network is, will occur. The revolution in television will continue. The search for viewers will become more intense as the fragmentation of the viewing audience continues.

After initially ignoring Turner and CNN and watching others spring up, the big three networks have finally starting counting—counting all of the viewers who turned us off and turned on those other guys, or even worse, turned off television altogether. In the process, the network television news programs were turned off, too. The network news shows almost always come on after the local news. Brokaw, Jennings, and Rather say "Good Evening" pretty much like Aimee, John, and Adele do in Denver and every other city in America with a local news anchor. One half hour started looking pretty much like every other half hour. Those flames on the local news looked exactly like the flames on network news. So why watch the local and national news? Many decided not to.

At the risk of sounding "typically network," there are some big distinctions between local and network news. Correspondents are typically older, more experienced, and better writers. We have "been there" and "done that," not once, but many times in different places across the globe. We think in broader terms. Our perspective is different. We can spend more time on a story. The networks can devote more resources to a story, both people and money, if that's what it takes. Because of a network's reach, our news stories usually involve more story telling than fact recital.

What about viewer loyalty? It doesn't exist, and probably never did after Cronkite and Huntley-Brinkley. The point was certainly driven home in 1995 with the buying and selling of local television stations across the country. For example, KCNC in Denver was the dominant local news station early evening and late when NBC sold the station in a four-market swap. The Denver station became a CBS affiliate, a kiss of death in 1995 with the eyeball network in the toilet in entertainment and news. When the switch happened, 20 percent of KCNC news viewers left. There was no loyalty, despite a local news operation that had the most admired anchor team, the best promotion, and the most community involvement.

The widely held notion that news was an obligation, a moral responsibility without regard to cost, also came to an end. The networks were sold to nonbroadcasters. Sold to General Electric. Sold to Tisch. Sold to Capitol Cities. The networks were money machines, and the news divisions, by god, were under the same obligation to produce a bottom line profit as sports, entertainment, and others. NBC went through a well documented, horrid, cost-cutting experience that nearly killed us. If you can believe it, the network news bureaus in the various cities were ordered not to buy the local newspaper. Too expensive! NBC lost 400 + workers. Correspondents were not renewed or replaced when contracts expired. Bureaus were downsized or closed. Equipment went to hell. We bought cheap junk and maintenance became nonexistent. The news divisions still haven't recovered. The number of employees in news is back at precut levels, but the distribution of those workers still leaves the news-gathering side of the equation shorthanded. The news magazine show, nonexistent during the austerity days, is where all of the new workers have gone. So the situation, while better, still leaves us without local papers.

As our viewers disappeared, so did our sense of direction. Like the popular book and movie, *The Hunt for Red October*, the networks were in "The Hunt for Numbers":

Who were the viewers we wanted? (young with buying power)

What happened? (They were not watching television

because the tube turned them off.)

When did they leave? (in the go-go 80s)

Where did they go? (to computers, to work, to play)

Why? (because the choices offered on the tube were mindless, out of touch, and off the mark to a generation of kids who saw the world through more than an 18-inch television screen in the living room. In the process of rejecting entertainment television, these viewers concluded the news was pretty mindless, often out of touch, and usually off the mark. The world kept going without Brokaw, Jennings, and Rather. In fact, the sun was often brighter without the evening din of Washington insider gossip, foreign crises, and generally bad news.)

How were the networks going to get those viewers back? (Well, that is still a question being answered, but the initial conclusions by news executives is what you see on television today.)

At a network level, it is amazingly similar to what local news operations have been serving up for years. When I started with NBC, the rule was that correspondents did not walk in stand-ups, flail our arms, point, wave or gesture. We stood still even if there was a freight train barreling down our backs. This stoic, statue-like pose conveyed a number of things to viewers. It provided no distractions to our words. It parlayed a certain importance to the title "correspondent." We had, as young reporters like to say, paid our dues. We were important, and our stature would not be diminished by walking around. As I get older, I'm also convinced the really old timers who had become bosses weren't sure their correspondents could walk and talk at the same time. For reasons I have yet to understand, all my bosses are old producers. There's not a reporter amongst the lot. It gnaws at me to watch some lunk who used to help correspondents put stories together become a know-it-all producer who, well, knows it all. But I digress. The issue was walking versus not walking.

Seeing was also an issue for awhile. One president of the news division decided he wanted his correspondents seen in every story they did. I had a personal rule that if the pictures were good, compelling, and told the story, why ruin them with my mug? After all, television is a medium of pictures and words. Pictures first, words second. Many young journalists never learned or remembered that in j-school. There's also another issue at play here. Most stand-ups are forced and are done to please news presidents or news directors. They are done to advance the careers of reporters, and they distract rather than add. The fact of the matter is most of us can't and don't think about the construction of a story while we are out in the field. Yet, we decide in the field that a stand-up is necessary. Reporters force the stand-up into the script because they have done a stand-up, and no matter how awkward, the stand-up will be included in the story.

Not long ago, the word went out to NBC correspondents that times had changed and movement was OK, indeed preferable. The trouble was most of us were too old to change. Most correspondents did nothing; some did try to walk a few steps, from point A to point B, for no reason other than to move. A few did the unthinkable. We actually tried to give meaning to movement. For example, if your walking took the viewer from one scene to another, "Wow," that was really special. If your walking evolved out of or into an effect, "Magnificent," we were really making progress now, and all of the producers who had become executive producers and senior producers were patting themselves on their backs for being so insightful, forward thinking, and downright visionary. Keep in mind, all of this walking stuff came from the correspondents. What came from the producers was, "Wow, magnificent!"

These orders of the day don't come as memos or directives or after conference calls where the executive producers explain what's behind their thinking. They just come, much like the wind. They also change, much like the wind. Correspondents have to figure out what the producers mean, really mean, when they say things like "Why don't you try . . ." or "That was really good." Does that mean you want us to do it all the time? Does that mean this is a new rule? Does it mean anything? Correspondents have to do a lot of interpreting when they get to the network.

A new buzzword has crept into the repertoire of executive producers and those who carry out their directives—"edge." It's a very dangerous word. Remember, though, we are in a search for viewers. Viewers need a reason to watch, keep watching, and turn the damn set on. The thinking goes that scripts with edge will accomplish this. It's a simple twist of a word or phrase that satisfies those who want the edge. Instead of, "The airport, with a couple of exceptions, operated efficiently in its first year of operation," a script with edge would read, "The airport failed several key tests after it opened, but did function as planned most of the time." This is slight of hand stuff that, in our quest for viewers, we try to justify (to ourselves mostly, but to viewers too who question our differing approach). Factually, the story is still accurate, but when it's edged, we are tricking, or trying to trick, the viewer. Emphasizing what's wrong before we say what's right is an approach viewers have long criticized. More importantly, it misses the real headline of the story. When we try to grab the viewer by hitting him over the head with a club of negatives, aren't we succumbing to the "bottom feeder" mentality?

Here's an example. The new Denver airport opened late and over budget, and in its first year got mostly negative attention from the national press, mainly me. I did stories for the network on the bungled baggage system, cracked runways, cracked tile in the terminal, a control tower where it snowed inside during a blizzard, air traffic controllers who took advantage of a government loophole and tried moving into new homes at taxpayer expense, and an airport where officials spent 15 million dollars of federal money because they would have had to give it back if the money wasn't spent. All of those stories were legitimate. When the airport's first-year anniversary neared, it was time to do an update. Two approaches were available—three big negatives or one positive. The negatives were the failed baggage system, a blizzard that almost closed the airport, which had been advertised and sold to the public as an all-weather facility, and a power surge that stranded hundreds of passengers because underground trains are the only way passengers get to and from the terminal and concourses. The positive angle was that the airport had become one of the most efficient in the country with on-time landings and departures. I should point out this was the reason the new Denver airport was built, to end the horrendous delays snowstorms caused at the old Denver airport. It was my decision to use the trifecta of negatives. It wasn't that the negatives outweighed the on-time performance record and, therefore, should be mentioned first. Rather, it was my thought—no, make that my conviction—based on years and years of dealing with New York producers over scripts that a negative approach had the edge they wanted. I knew it would be smooth sailing with script approval by going negative first. Both approaches were legitimate. But the news was an airport that worked, that had become a leader and was accomplishing its mission. Negative won out over positive. The airport anniversary story had a better edge, but good journalism lost.

I'll admit it. Maybe I've lost the edge. Perhaps I'm too old and don't want to change. I liked the old school of journalism a lot better than the new. Perhaps edge is what's needed to get viewers back and attract new ones. Maybe absolute balance isn't necessary anymore. The magazine shows, old and new, have certainly attracted an audience without that as a cornerstone. However, what is of concern is, if the so-called straight news shows adopt this more liberal approach to news, where are viewers suppose to get news without bias? I'm afraid, not on television. I liked the old way. Stories were, in my view, better balanced. When we didn't worry about what a story cost, whether it fit the label, or whether it was constructed with edge, it was much easier to get the Who,

What, Where, When, Why, and How's answered. It was much easier to present the material in a straightforward, balanced way. Both sides of every story were presented. Storytellers need that balance to weave the intrigue, the controversy, the mystery that almost every story presents. It's not, "Just the facts, ma'am!" It was journalism.

Then what is "The Fleecing of America"? It is dangerous and controversial journalism. It is, I'm afraid, the direction journalism is headed. It is news with attitude. It is commentary. But, it is not labeled as such. "Fleecing" began on NBC in late 1995. It is an attempt to expose fraud, waste, and abuse of taxpayer money. The concept is sound; the idea, noble; the subject matter, rich. My concern begins with the name. It defines an attitude that runs counter to the practice of journalism. It has never been our job to take sides, but that's what "Fleecing" does right from the get-go. When a "Fleecing" report is introduced, everyone watching NBC knows NBC is taking a position. There is no middle ground or extenuating circumstances. It's black and white. Good guys and bad guys. Where the name came from is a mystery to me.

Don't get confused. We do a ton of research and reject many more ideas than we take on. For those stories that do air, the evidence is clear and overwhelming. They are good investigative reports. What they fail to do is provide the same kind of balance that other nonlabeled stories get—the kind of balance and fairness that placed news reportering among the most respected of professions, not "bottom feeders." Our slide in respectability has come quickly; in part, because of the junk news shows on the air, but also because the legitimate news organizations are letting their own standards slip in our search for viewers. Our job used to be to present the news.

The reaction to "Fleecing" has been predictable. It's a very successful franchise, and my guess is that it attracts viewers. It's based on the same premise as *60 Minutes*. Almost everyone thinks his or her tax money is being wasted, so to see confirmation of that on the national news, well, that's satisfaction. On the other hand, "Fleecing" has also generated a good deal of hate letters, accusatory fingers, and negative side effects.

The "Fleecing" that produced the most e-mail ever to NBC was a spot I did on a little bird in southern Arizona. The government has been trying for many years to reintroduce the ringed-neck bobwhite quail to this part of the country. About 800 million dollars has been spent, but the birds must not like the area south of Tucson, because they keep dying before they reproduce. We labeled this a fleece. What started as a quail project had become a national wildlife sanctuary. We labeled that "mission creep." What originally was a U.S. effort began spilling over into Mexico where the bird has always done better and where it still does today. Mexico is its principal habitat. Southern Arizona is on the outer fringe of that. Well, my oh my, get out of the way because you'd think we just attacked motherhood, apple pie, and the Confederacy. The e-mail came, and it didn't stop. Not one, 10 or 20 letters, but 52 in the first days after the report aired. We were accused of attacking the Endangered Species Act, buckling under to the so-called "Wise Use Movement," and how dare NBC suggest that environmental issues should be quick fixes that a little taxpayers' money will cure. Some of the e-mail was organized and attempted to make it seem like we had offended half the universe. A certain department at a certain university started typing, and after 11 letters were sent, they quit. I'd name the university, but we may do a "Fleecing" on them, and I don't want to tip my hand. Of most concern though was the tone of almost all of the e-mail. It took us to task for presenting an issue that the letter writers thought was one-sided. NBC was accused of deciding in advance that the quail project was a waste of taxpayers' money. One of the things I've tried not to forget is the intelligence of the viewer. "Fleecing," I'm afraid, ignores that.

"Fleecing" is also hurting us in another way, a far more serious consequence that could hurt our efforts to gather the facts. For more than 13 years, I have been putting together environmental stories. Within that community of folks, I had earned a pretty good reputation. I was considered fair-minded and evenhanded in presenting stories that dealt with the environment. Realistically, I was considered a friend of those who were advancing the cause of living in harmony with all of God's creatures on this earth. From the forests to the rivers to the mountains, NBC, with my signature attached, has aired hundreds of stories about those issues. At the same time, I've been able to forge alliances with those groups and individuals who use the land: miners, lumberjacks, and developers. It has been a delicate balancing act, but by being fair and balanced, I have managed not to alienate. As such, I could count on both sides of this often contentious issue letting me know when some event was going to occur—a protest here, a community meeting there, a hearing somewhere else—providing the glue to develop dozens of good stories that NBC would not have known about until after the fact. Sources! I could also count on government officials faxing releases to our offices and, more importantly, taking my phone calls, usually without delay. Those government sources provided the national perspective to otherwise local stories. They had the numbers to support the argument or premise of many stories. They knew they could talk off-the-record without fear. They usually had or knew where to look or knew where I could look to find the Who, What, Where, When, Why, and How. They were, and still are, invaluable to our gathering of facts. Without their help, the job of telling the story gets infinitely tougher.

And that has started to happen, largely I'm afraid, because of "Fleecing." The word is out in government, in the environmental community, in the user groups. Instead of "Hi, how are you?", now it's, "Is this going to be a 'Fleecing of America' report?" Some people have refused to talk. Some are hesitant. Still others let it be known they didn't like that last "Fleecing," and their tone becomes guarded when new questions are asked about other stories. As a reporter, I have lost some credibility. It's not that the "Fleecing" reports are inaccurate, wrong, or that they shouldn't be done. It's the damn name that's hurting, and the approach each "Fleecing" has to take because of the name. It's the label that removes the fairness that sources had come to depend on. It's the approach the stories take that removes the balance both sides were able to live with before. We're not reporting the same way. We're reporting with attitude. Before the search for viewers started, before the bottom line came into play, before we needed edge in our reports, we didn't do it that way.

So where does that leave us? I would propose that the news business on both a national and local level is slipping down a slippery slope to mediocrity. Our values aren't as strong. The foundation is weakened. Rather than trying to shore up the base that served journalism so well for so many years, we are trying to build the pile higher. In almost every local newscast, there is a self-help report, a giveaway, a trouble-shooter report responding to consumer complaints. There's a specialist this and a specialist that. Labels, labels, labels. Where's the news? It's there, but in 15-second readers, voice-overs, or cutesy little one-liners. The news is being shortchanged for the labels. We are responding to trends in the marketplace as fast as our viewers change from one fad to the other. We report what's on the surface, but not what's below it. Well, there always used to be enough time. At least that's my sense of it. The newscast hasn't changed. Thirty minutes is still nineteen minutes of news after the commercials. That hasn't changed. What's shortened the broadcast is the labels. Those are the stories that get the time the other news can't. Those are the stories that have been promoted. Those are the stories we are building the newscast around.

The newscast is in search of viewers. The newscast is trying to be timely and responsive to trends by being trendy. The newscast is trying to resurrect itself by copying what others do better. The newscast has lost its way. It is, I'm afraid, why we are thought of as Bottom Feeders.

3

The Network Correspondent as Historian, Diplomat, Student, and Vampire

Walter C. Rodgers

R eporters have been traditionally stereotyped as bloodsuckers by Hollywood, and there is some validity to this celluloid image. Perhaps "vampire" is more appropriate. A television correspondent is a subspecies whose hours are not dissimilar to those of vampires and whose quarry has certain parallels. We thrive on blood, whether it is the politician wounded by scandal, wars in Bosnia, or suicide bombings in Israel. The adage, "If it bleeds, it leads," however gruesome, remains the stuff of which television news is about. And, like the vampire of myth, once bitten, there is no turning back.

My first bite came on August 4, 1964, when I was working between semesters as a freelance soundman. We were suddenly sent to the Pentagon for an urgent briefing by then Defense Secretary Robert McNamara who announced that the U.S. Destroyers *Maddox* and *Turner* had been attacked by North Vietnamese torpedo boats in the Gulf of Tonkin. This battle, which may never have occurred, became chapter one of the Vietnam War. McNamara was pointing at charts and maps and my adrenaline was pumping, as it has ever since when something historic, important, or interesting happens. The following autumn I was enrolled in a doctoral program in history at the University of Washington, but my heart was never in it. Sitting in the bowels of the UW library writing papers on American constitutional history, I realized that I had been bitten: I did not want to study history any more. I wanted to live it.

Before the advent of the foreign correspondent, history was recorded by the winners or the occasional dispassionate observer like Herodotus. With occasional exceptions, the losers tended to be victims who, if they survived, were too busy trying to feed themselves to worry about how posterity would remember their plight. In the late twentieth century, the historian's traditional role of keeping track of societies' winners and losers has fallen to the television correspondent. We are witnessing not so much the end of history as the birth of an instant history—recorded on videotape, not by scholars but by whiz-kids whose critical faculties fall far short of those of the traditional scholar, if for no other reason than that they do not have the historian's opportunity for reflection.

The network correspondent, and more often than not the foreign correspondent, has become the scribe, or purveyor, of this instant history. Instant history is the hand that has been dealt the television correspondent by technology, and we must play it out for better or for worse. Because of this technology, future historical scholars may simply be overwhelmed. Instead of trying to piece together the picture of an era from fragments of the past, future historians may be writing eclectically from a surfeit of video tapes and computer data. In addition to the traditional primary sources of manuscripts, diaries, and letters to analyze, there will be thousands of hours of videotape to screen, these being but a fragment of what was recorded, because most of the outtakes will have been thrown away. The scholar of the next age will be drawing conclusions from neatly produced video packages, the products of the winners of the age of technology.

No future scholar, however disdainful he or she may be of television, can in good conscience ignore this resource. At no previous moment in history can the historian do what the network television correspondent can now do today, namely, insert a shooting cassette and screen and rescreen a historical event. I screened and rescreened the Brezhnev and Andropov funerals. Had I been prescient enough at the time to read the historical tea leaves I was screening, it might have been possible to predict the ascendance of Mikhail Gorbachev in the Soviet Union a year before he was elected by the Politburo. When Soviet President Yuri Andropov died more than a year earlier, the videotapes showed an extraordinarily confident, if not brash, woman rushing forward from a delegation of official mourners in Red Square to place a red carnation on Andropov's bier. Such an impulsive act was antithetical to the Russian character, unless, of course, your name is Raisa Gorbachev, and you are married to the man who a year later was to become general secretary of the Communist Party of the Soviet Union. No one stopped her. This is the stuff of which good history could and should be written, and if future historians ignore this technology, their work will be the poorer for it.

There is, however, an inherent danger to the new instant historians in this process. One can become so consumed in the screening of an event that it becomes impossible to determine the fact of having witnessed a video sequence from the fiction of having merely scripted it. The true witness is the camera's lens, behind which is a shooter, who sees an event with only one eye behind a viewfinder, and that is reflected on the retina only in black and white. Correspondents may or may not see what the tape records, for they may be looking in a different direction from the camera. The tape editor is probably never an eyewitness to the event but only the assembler of the video puzzle. Nonetheless, a future scholar drawing on the resources of a network television correspondent's report will have the advantage of seeing at least some of the event and perhaps dissecting it with his own eyes. He must be ever mindful that he is working through and with secondary source material. It should never be forgotten that it is in the nature of video to distort images as well as record them. In the early 1980s, television correspondents could with their naked eye see that Moscow, the capital of the other Superpower, was literally crumbling—prefiguring the collapse of an empire. But the camera was too limited to capture this broader image swept up by the correspondent's eye, and the story went unreported.

Just as important to remember is that the videotape image records but a 45-degree fraction of any event at any given time. Written history has ever been at least as limited and subjective. Read United States history before the Civil Rights Revolution of the 1960s, and you will find precious little record of black history in a country that had a substantial slave population for more than 200 years prior to the American Civil War. History is ever being reinterpreted, and now that interpretation has fallen to the video whiz-kids. Gore Vidal shrewdly observed, "He who screens the history, makes the history."

That may not be as bad as it seems on the face of it. Between the period when only "winners" were recording history, and the advent of the instant historians of the era of television news, there were occasions during the post-Enlightenment when the "losers" were permitted to write history, with tragic consequences. With much magnanimity, the reunited American Republic permitted the children of the Confederacy to write and perpetuate their own version of the American Civil War that resulted in a shading of history and perpetuated racism. For 100 years after that horrible war, children of the American South were raised to believe in the "glorious cause," while ignoring the fact that that cause perpetuated the most evil of institutions: human slavery.

The Bosnian example is the second to leap to mind. The Serbs are among history's perpetual losers, who have been allowed to turn their repeated defeats and tragedies into a sacred cause. While Serbs were undoubtedly victims, the repeated telling of their victimization has transformed their national consciousness into a messianic quest for revenge.

Fortunately, the advent of instant history and the courageous reporting of network television correspondents have greatly limited the spread of the cancer of the losers version of history. Not much of the rest of the world subscribes to the Serbs' perversion of reality, thanks to correspondents, cameramen and women, and producers who risked their lives and on some cases paid with them, to record the new techno-history on videotape.

Still, not all of any event can be squeezed into a videotape cameo, even with the advantage of 24-hour television news services like CNN. Often the most telling absurdities have to be omitted because of this limited news window. I recall a conversation with a Serb militiaman guarding a checkpoint outside Sarajevo in the winter of 1994. Several days earlier he had held a nine-millimeter pistol to my head and informed me he was going to pull the trigger because he was vexed with my reporting on CNN. (The Serb government in Belgrade routinely took reports in English, translating them into Serbo-Croatian with a government twist that showed the Western media as maligning and lying about the Serbs in order to produce widespread paranoia. My report had been repaired with me appearing on camera but with a Serb voice-over saying things I had never said. It was small wonder the gunman at the checkpoint was enraged.) For whatever reasons, he deemed it imprudent to execute me at that time. During a second encounter at his checkpoint several days later, he invited me into his bunker to watch him consume several glasses of moonshine brandy. After he mellowed, he asked me, "Do you know how it feels to have your grandmother raped by the Turks 400 years ago?" It was too difficult to explain there were no American grandmothers 400 years ago.

The single advantage video techno-historians have over what has gone before is that they represent neither the winner nor the loser. They report on both the victor and the vanquished, often one on one day, and the other the next. Professional historians, academics, may argue that they bring no prejudices to the craft, but evidence suggests quite the contrary. There have been whole classes of Marxist historians, even in the West, and an earlier generation of white Ivy League academicians who ignored black history as unworthy. This is not to suggest that the instant historians are not without their agendas. They run the same risk of advocacy journalism that confronted the more ideological historians of this century. Still, it should be noted that without these video whiz-kids of companies like CNN, the Kurds would have been just another forgotten ethnic group obliterated by Saddam Hussein; South Africa would probably still have a white minority government; and today's Bosnian Muslims would have been another forgotten example of genocide. Thus, the techno-historian television correspondent goes beyond the scholar's traditional role of reflective recording of history to become a crusader for peoples who have no other ombudsman.

Time and technology have produced this evolution in the foreign correspondent's portfolio, from the days when Rudyard Kipling was penning his reports from India for readers in London. We have forsaken the pad and pencil of Ernie Pyle for the computer. The very term "foreign correspondent" has become an oxymoron. Nothing is foreign when one's image is electronically projected simultaneously into brokerage houses in London, Delhi, Tokyo, Sydney, and New York. Technology, with its satellites, computers, and cable television, has made all correspondents in varying degrees both international and local. It is possible to work for a global company like CNN, be based in Jerusalem, and walk down the streets of Riyadh, and have people pull their cars to a stop at curbside, get out and say, "Hey, I know you. I liked your coverage of the Rabin assassination."

Global television has taken a quantum leap forward. While most Americans were watching Rather, Brokaw, and Jennings, the rest of the English-speaking world beyond the United States was watching global television. The United States comprises 4.5 percent of the global population. But 20 percent of the rest of the globe's 5 billion inhabitants speak English, and satellites are beaming CNNI (CNN's Cable News Network International) into the Defense Ministry in Baghdad, the Foreign Ministry in Lima, and ordinary households around the world. In Israel, one survey showed 28 percent of the population watches CNN at least once a day. The percentage of Americans tuning into any one of the major North American evening news broadcasts is probably lower than that.

The worldwide audience of CNN International and BBC World is impossible to quantify. Most Americans are unaware these global networks exist because unless they have their own home satellite dishes, they are not generally commercially available on domestic cable systems. However, the value of this global approach to television is not lost on the U.S. government. CNN International is beamed round the clock into the State Department, the Pentagon, and the CIA, as well as in other government agencies where there is an absolute need to know. Although it would be disingenuous to describe the CNNI and BBC programming as intellectual, the audience tends to be highbrow and government elites. The reach and power of these global news-gathering organizations is awesome, even if it is not recognized in the American heartland.

One example of this reach was in February 1994 when I was in Sarajevo. The Serbs fired a large mortar shell into a crowded marketplace where several hundred half-starved people gathered to buy whatever food was available. Sixty-eight people were killed in what became a massacre. A few weeks later I was in Moscow and attended an invitation-only news conference by Foreign Minister Andrei Kozerev. Before the conference began, a friend from ABC News Moscow and I were chatting, and she snidely asked, "Who watches CNN outside of people in hotel rooms?" I told her about Bosnian Muslims who, after seeing my reporting, would approach me on the streets of Sarajevo and thank me for "telling the world" about their tragedy. One even kissed my hand and thanked me for helping them. My ABC Moscow friend was unimpressed. During the course of Mr. Kozerev's news conference, I asked a question about the Russian role in negotiations to bring a settlement in the Bosnian civil war. The Russian foreign minister recognized me from my reporting from Sarajevo, stopped his news conference, and proceeded to tell the gathering what an important service I had performed for the international community in my reporting out of Sarajevo several weeks earlier. Kozerev said the world owed CNN a debt of gratitude for its coverage of the marketplace massacre, and he extolled my coverage to my colleagues for another three minutes. Afterwards I approached my former colleague from ABC News and asked, "Does that tell you who watches CNN?"

In the Middle East, I know that the Israeli prime minister, the Syrian president, the Egyptian president, the king of Jordan, and Saddam Hussein all watch CNN. What we report about the Israeli-Palestinian struggle is viewed with avid interest throughout the rest of the Islamic world by the educated English-speaking classes. The power, as well as the recognition factor, of the international correspondent in this age of satellites has taken a quantum leap from the days when Morley Safer was reporting on burning villages in Vietnam. Then, it facilitated an American exodus from an ill-considered and unpopular war. Today, news coverage from organizations like CNN has persuaded an American president, if not the public, to accept the injection of 20,000 U.S. troops into the Bosnian conflict.

It is ever a shock, even for those in the industry, to realize the power of the new technology in the hands of news organizations and individual journalists. The late British publisher Robert Maxwell was a true prophet in this technological revolution. We shared seats on the same British Airways flight from Moscow to London in 1984 in the depths of the Cold War. Maxwell had had several meetings in the Kremlin discussing the impact of satellite television broadcasts and satellite dish technology with Soviet Central Committee members. I clearly recall him telling me that old Kremlin hard-liners were "quaking in their boots" because they knew technology was soon to make a mockery of their attempts to hermetically seal information coming into the then closed Soviet Union. Before anyone heard terms like "Glasnost" and "Peristroika," Maxwell was predicting the old Soviet Union would come unglued because its managers would soon lose their iron grip on the Russian people because of VCRs and satellite dishes. It was not until several years later that I realized how visionary our conversation was. I was fortunate to have been there when the evil empire began to unravel, in no small way as the result of the implications of the technology Maxwell understood. Governments could still maintain their monopolies over their own news, but satellites had rendered those monopolies porous.

It is a function of the power of the new global television entities that the network correspondent's role has been expanded from a recorder of events to a quasi-diplomatic role, sadly, often with celebrity status. The latter is most regrettable because the power of television is so seductive; too frequently correspondents come to believe they are bigger than the story, or worse, that they are the story. It is an easy trap to fall into. A truism of our times is, "Presidents come and presidents go, but the Sam Donaldsons and Dan Rathers seem to go on forever." The pseudo-omniscience of this stardom is as fatal to good journalism as it is to good historical research.

In the days of the Cold War, the Soviet Embassy in Washington videotaped the evening news programs in the United States and flew them in the diplomatic pouch to the Foreign Ministry in Moscow the following day for analysis. A lesson of how closely the foreign correspondent's work is scrutinized by a host government was brought home most vividly at the first Reagan-Gorbachev Summit in Geneva in late autumn 1986. Having been recognized to ask a question at Gorbachev's news conference, I began by introducing myself as Walter Rodgers of ABC News. Gorbachev interrupted me brusquely, saying, "Yes, we know who you are." (In the days of the U.S./Soviet bipolar world, it should have come as no surprise that the leader of the other superpower should know the resident correspondent from ABC. Today, although I am certain the Russian president knows the CNN correspondents, it is doubtful that he could name the ABC correspondent in Moscow. Sadly this is a function of ABC, CBS, and NBC largely ceding international news coverage to CNN and BBC. The big three American networks, in believing the American public wants only domestic news, have marginalized themselves and have become provincial in the greater sweep of global news organizations. This same vignette also illustrates how television turns correspondents into internationally recognized celebrities, if not peripheral players.) My question to the Soviet leader was simple, "Do you believe the world is a safer place, after your meeting with President Reagan?" Gorbachev used my question after this first Superpower Summit since 1979 to defuse the doomsday sorts of the Reagan years. He said the world had backed away from the brink of nuclear war because of his "fireside chat" with the U.S. president. His response to my question was banner headlines in every paper in Europe, and many in the United States.

This celebrity status forced upon the television correspondent by the influence wielded by his medium confers a quasi-diplomatic rank of no mean proportion. It is little short of diplomatic immunity. Besides opening doors, it sometimes puts television correspondents above the law, and it carries a currency of its own. The danger is that as power corrupts, so does the power of television and sometimes absolutely. On occasion, it turns an honest reporter into a dishonest celebrity. In a brilliant essay, veteran *Washington Post* correspondent Richard Harwood wrote of TV news celebrities, "The more prominent today's star journalists become, the more they are forced to give up the essence of real journalism, which is the search for information. . . . their jobs provide them with neither the time nor the opportunity to do the research, reading and reporting required to make sense of the news . . . to give it meaning and perspective. And because of the perpetual race for ratings, they are often under pressure to entertain rather than inform."

At times when I was the ABC News bureau chief in Moscow at the height of the Cold War, and now to a lesser degree as CNN bureau chief in Jerusalem, even a quasi-celebrity status as a television correspondent confers a kind of diplomatic rank. In Moscow, I often felt like the diplomatic liaison between corporate headquarters and the government of the country in which I worked. In Jerusalem, one of my first tasks was to repair a rupture that had occurred during CNN's coverage of the Palestinian Intifada, which had led to our being virtually banned from the prime minister's office. Like a new ambassador presenting his credentials to a head of state, I made an appointment to see the late Israeli Prime Minister Yitzhak Rabin's chief aide, Eitan Haber. He proceeded to berate one of my CNN predecessors in terms that combined the foulest epithets in English, Hebrew, and Yiddish. He openly threatened to shut down our bureau and vowed he would personally kill my predecessor if this person ever stepped foot in Israel again. This minicrisis was defused with unexpected ease. The inspiration came from a line from the Hebrew prophet Jeremiah, which I quoted: "The fathers have eaten sour grapes and the children's teeth are set on edge. Ye shall not have occasion to use this proverb, no not any more in all Israel." So stunned was the prime minister's aide that a Gentile could extemporaneously quote the Old Testament to him that all hostility toward CNN melted.

An earlier example of the correspondent/bureau chief playing a quasi-diplomatic role was considerably more excruciating. In 1986, ABC's Entertainment Division produced a docudrama called *AMERIKA*, a badly conceived, abominably executed, three-part television series about a Soviet occupation of a heartland American town. The best efforts of the News

Division of Capital Cities/ABC to stop this project were to no avail. These were the Reagan years, where arch-conservatives like their Secretary of Education Bill Bennett attached political significance to what was simply a poor programming decision.

At ground zero in the heart of the "evil empire," it was anything but a trifle. The Central Committee of the Communist Party of the Soviet Union was moving quickly to expel me as the ABC correspondent and close down the ABC Bureau there. Pleas for help from the News Division's management ultimately resulted in a "you're on your own" on this one. There had been hours and hours of negotiations with the Soviet Foreign Ministry, which, incidentally, knew about the *AMERIKA* program before I ever did. I was summoned in for an explanation, not unlike a foreign ambassador.

What evolved was a serious rift between the News and Entertainment Divisions of ABC. The News Division fought the project because it was aware of the thinly veiled threat from the Soviet government to shut down its Moscow Bureau if the program aired. The Entertainment Division had support from Reagan Conservatives who saw the entire matter as an American network caving into the demands of the Evil Empire. The simple truth was that the Entertainment Division's ratings were so low they grasped at any straw. (Curiously, ABC had an interesting ally in this minicrisis in the form of the Soviet Foreign Ministry, which apparently wanted to avoid the pettiness and embarrassment of shutting down a major American television network's bureau in Moscow).

As the crisis came to a climax, I received an urgent call to rush to the Foreign Ministry. I was asked to prepare a letter to the Central Committee explaining the difference between the Entertainment and News Divisions of the network. It was an exercise combining the wisdom of an Aesop's fable and the wisdom of Russian folk proverbs. I never bothered to clear the official letter with the News Division in New York, which had already told me I was "on my own." My letter simply explained that it is possible for the son of the same parent to be innocent of the wrongs committed by his sibling. The Babushkas on the Moscow streets would have seen the logic of it, and fortunately the hotheads of the Central Committee did, too. Within 24 hours, a friend from the Foreign Ministry telephoned to inform me my letter had defused the bid to shut down ABC News in Moscow. I suspect that cooler heads in the Soviet government also prevailed because someone had the good sense to realize that closing an American news bureau would have played directly into the hands of the most rabid Red-baiting Reaganites.

Even if one is not a bureau chief and has the good fortune to be merely a correspondent, one cannot escape these pressures, especially in the Middle East. There, the ideological lines between Arab and Jew are so rigidly drawn there seems no happy middle ground. You are either "for them" or "agin' them." The correspondent's diplomatic portfolio does have its limits. Milton Berle once quipped, "Diplomacy is the art of skating on thin ice without getting into deep water." But the old journalist saw, "If they like you, you aren't doing your job," requires the correspondent to wade in several fathoms deep, "diplomacy be damned."

In the weeks before Christmas 1995, I filed what I considered an interesting, but innocuous, story on the plight of the Palestinian Christian minority, living in Bethlehem in the face of an increasingly hostile Islamic radical movement, Hamas, which comprised at least 25 percent of Bethlehem's population. I had worked the story hard, walking the streets for two hours before we ever brought a camera into town, trying to win the confidence of local Christian Palestinian businessmen. Virtually no one would talk on the record, but on background they told alarming stories of desecration of family graves, personal harassment, fist fights with Muslims, and de facto economic boycotts.

The Palestinian victim mentality raised howls from their widespread Diaspora, for the report ruptured the myth of Palestinian unity and Pan-Arab brotherhood. Reaction from the Palestinian Authority was as heavy-handed and clumsy as anything that came out of Eastern Europe in the Cold War. A Palestinian bureaucrat threatened to cancel my credentials and published an unsigned letter denouncing me and calling me a tool of "hostile, Zionist, right-wing circles." A message went out over the Internet decrying my report as "CNN's poison," excoriating me and avowing I was a liar. Another letter was sent to my boss, Ted Turner, calling me an "embarrassment" to CNN.

The following month the right-wing *Jerusalem Post* ran a headline, "CNN Atones for Rare Boldness." Next, the Israel right was after me, claiming that after filing this initially "bold report," I had caved in to the Palestinians in a later interview with Hannarl Ashrawi, a member of the Palestinian Council. What the *Jerusalem Post* neglected to point out, however, was that my interview with Ashrawi was conducted in Bethlehem on Christmas Eve and was essentially about Christmas Eve festivities.

The incident demonstrates that in an age of global television, no story is innocuous. Secondly, it is a reminder that the network correspondent is always a student. When you get to the point in your career that nothing is new, get out of the business. The correspondent is ever the quick study, and television news demands many of the same skills needed in university: the ability to do research and communicate, specifically, to speak and write clearly. Good reporting also requires constant study, research, and immersion in your story, just as one immerses oneself in a seminar. Most importantly, it demands you read everything: newspapers, magazines, scholarly journals, and books.

During my five years in Moscow for ABC, I used the entire experience as a graduate seminar in twentieth-century Russian studies. The only books I read were about Russia, the only literature, Russian. I spent hundreds of hours interviewing Russians, from Communist Party officials to cab drivers to scholars, children of the purges, survivors of the siege of Leningrad, and veterans of Stalingrad. It made me a better correspondent, and I continue to use that same approach to my current assignment in the Middle East. Every assignment for the overseas correspondent should be a learning experience: a seminar in African Studies, Russian Studies, the Far East, or the Middle East. The energy level of a university undergraduate married to the discipline of a graduate student are the ingredients of which good television journalists are made. The camera betrays few things more quickly than a correspondent's ennui. The camera reflects the degree of authority, enthusiasm, and intellectual interest a correspondent brings to a story. It all adds up to credibility, and bluff has about the same life span in live television that it has on a university examination. An active curiosity about everything helps make a good reporter. Never tire of asking, "Why?" A good student and a good reporter always challenge the accepted wisdom.

Nobody will ever like you in the Middle East. The most you can hope for is respect. This is a story in which everyone thinks they are the good guy—a view that is reinforced by the divine conviction that God is on their side. In such a climate, it is well not to assume one is more than a student with much to learn. Objectivity, such as it is, becomes solely the province of the student/correspondent, because everyone else in the region has a divine bias.

In the Middle East currently, one covers Jewish religious students who assassinate prime ministers because they believe God told them to violate the Commandment, "Thou shalt not kill." More than a few Rabbis actually advocated political assassination to preserve Biblical Israel. Muslim clerics send young boys out to die with dynamite strapped around their waists, telling them it is Allah's will. These same boys are promised "72 virgins waiting for them in Paradise" if only they will kill a Jew. Their suicides, outlawed by the Koran, are justified by these high priests of hate as an honorable death, a "Jihad," or Holy War against the enemies of Islam, namely Israelis. While their brains, hands, and legs lie charred and black in bloodstained streets, these same boys' families and friends venerate them. Some dream of emulating them.

Amid such righteousness and certitude, the correspondent who covers the Middle East is well served in thinking of himself as little more than a student who heeds the counsel of the Prophet Micah: "Do justly, love mercy, and walk humbly with thy God."

4

Science, Race, and Network News

George Strait

Race has always played a central role in my career. The task for me and any black professional is to not let race define my career. I got my first job in broadcasting because I was the first person to walk through the door of WQXI, a rock-and-roll radio station in Atlanta, who had a college degree (actually I had a master's degree), who could read and speak English clearly (that was determined by reading commercial copy for a supermarket chain), and was black. It was 1969, the station was up for FCC license renewal, and it needed to integrate its on-air staff. I got my big break in television news because when the news director at WPVI in Philadelphia needed to integrate his staff, a disc jockey I had worked with in Atlanta said, "I know this kid in Atlanta. . . ." Before I left Atlanta, my boss asked, "Do you know anybody to replace you?" I said, "I know this kid just out of college. . . ." He was hired, and one of the first networks of black journalists began. It wasn't an "ol' boy" network just yet, but it was evidence that who you know is often more important than what you know.

From the time I started work in Philadelphia in 1972, I wanted to go to the network. I made two serious tries, sending resume reels, submitting to interviews, getting recommendations, but each time I was told, "Not yet." By 1976, I had left Philadelphia and gone to Washington, D.C., working for the CBS bureau that covered Capitol Hill for CBS's five owned and operated stations. It wasn't the network, but it was close. In 1977, a coincidence of two events gave me my shot. During a round of budget cuts, CBS closed the bureau, which voided my contract, and ABC fired its black correspondent, the late Bill Matney, one of the black pioneers in network news. ABC approached Ed Bradley. He had just been offered a job at *60 Minutes*, so he said, "I can't do it, but I know this good young reporter. . . ." In October 1977, I began. At that time, I was one of only seven African-Americans reporting the news on network television.

There was a bit of self-consciousness between the networks and their black air personalities during those early days. Soon after Ed Bradley went to *60 Minutes*, he sent a memo to the executive producer, Don Hewitt, informing him that from then on he would be calling himself by his new Muslim name, Abdul Salim Muhammed (or something like that). Hewitt didn't know what to do. He didn't want to offend his new correspondent or his audience. He was visibly relieved to learn Ed was joking. Soon after I joined ABC, there was a race riot in Bermuda. Before sending me, my bosses went out of their way to assure me that race was not the primary reason why I was being sent but that race did play a role in their decision. I told them my interests were so broad that I wouldn't let myself be ghettoized. As evidence, during my first year at ABC I did so many stories about farmers, crop prices, and agriculture policy that I became known as the farm expert. Pretty good for a kid from the city. Getting away from Washington, working with camera crews from around the country, and delivering longer stories with a look that was different and more stylized than the traditional network piece raised my profile in ways that would not have been possible if I had stayed within the beltway.

For a black TV reporter, being on the road in the Midwest had its moments. I remember I was in Dodge City, Kansas, and discovered that I had forgotten my hair pick. Remember the ol' Afro hair pick blacks used to comb their hair? I went to the local drug store, asked for a hair pick, and they directed me to the toothpicks. I asked if there was another drug store in town, one from a national chain. That store didn't know what I was talking about either. On my way back to the hotel, I passed a store that sold barbecue supplies. I found and bought a big wooden fork used to toss salad. I didn't dare to go looking for some "Afro sheen."

My early career at ABC had the normal highs and lows and the same idiosyncratic reasons for success and failure. My first low occurred after a report I filed for *Good Morning America (GMA)* about the riots in Bermuda. My sixties militancy showed when I referred to the rioters as "brave revolutionaries." At that time, most ABC affiliates used stories from *GMA* for their news broadcasts at noon. One local news director objected to my characterization and wrote a scathing letter to the executive producer of *GMA*. He agreed and refused to let me on his broadcast for a number of weeks. Because *GMA* was my primary outlet during that time, it was a severe and deserved reprimand. I was rehabilitated by a silly story I did for the evening show, *World News Tonight*. It was springtime in Washington—time for the annual rite of watching to see if the pandas at the National Zoo would successfully mate. Because of previous failures, that year they imported a male from England, gave him Sing Sing's cage, Sing Sing's feed, and Sing Sing's woman. You get the point. The anchor, Frank Reynolds, giggled (and he wasn't a giggler); the control room was in stitches. I was a hero and a serious player again.

Life around the bureau was uneventful. Some of my coworkers saw me as just another reporter, another rookie. Some saw me as someone who got a special break. Some saw my lows as evidence that I didn't belong; others saw my highs as vindication for my hiring. Outwardly, there was no racism; there rarely is. The biggest problem was that I felt lonely. There were no other black reporters, editors, or producers to commiserate with.

One producer was especially salty. He was a salty sort anyway, but toward me there was a keen edge. It was always confusing to me because he was my senior by only a few months. What's a producer? The smart answer is they are responsible for making correspondents look good. They do much of the logistical planning, editorial research, and sit with the tape editor physically constructing a story. Correspondents get all of the credit for a story; producers get most of the responsibility. Producers advance to become heads of divisions and networks. Correspondents advance to better stories and beats.

Early one afternoon we got word that there had been a disaster in West Virginia—a big smokestack had collapsed killing 60 people, 30 from the same family. I was sent to cover the family angle; another reporter and that salty producer were sent to cover the accident. The time pressure was intense. We went on the air at six o'clock, but we didn't leave Washington until one. I landed at two, but the disaster was 150 miles from where we had to edit and feed the story. My crew and I hustled deep into the hollows of West Virginia, miles from where we had landed. There were four of us: me, a white cameraman, a black female sound tech, and a six-foot seven-inch, black lighting tech.

We must have been quite a sight to the folks who saw us coming around that mountain. When we got to the main house, there was a man outside standing there with a shotgun. He would not let us in. "I said 'no.' We're grieving." When he moved the barrel of his gun toward us, I knew he was serious. But I had to speak to somebody. I asked, "Are those your grandparents sitting on the porch across the street?" When he said yes, we went to their home. They had no guard and shared their grief with us, as well as the family photos of the men who died. It was now three-thirty. When we rushed back to the airplane, it was four-fifteen. We took off and an hour later landed in Charleston. My New York office said it had arranged for a driver to take us to the hotel where we would edit and feed the story to air. As we ran off the plane, a woman rushed up to us and said our car was over here. As she sped toward town, she said, "I am sure glad you boys work for CBS. I love that Walter Cronkite." I said, "I love him, too." We got to the hotel at five-thirty, finished editing at five-fifty eight, and showed a moving story about death, tragedy, and how families pull together to America at three minutes after six. That salty producer edited the story that ran before mine. While having a beer after the broadcast, he acknowledged that I had done a good job and was OK. "I guess you are qualified," he said. We never became friends, but at that moment, we did become colleagues.

About 18 months after I was hired, ABC offered me a chance to cover the White House. I wasn't the lead correspondent there—that title went to an irascible, dogged correspondent named Sam Donaldson. I would be the third of three correspondents. My responsibilities would be to report to ABC radio, the weekend report, and *GMA*. It was low profile but a place ABC put young reporters who showed promise. It was only the second time in history that a black reporter with any profile had covered the White House for a network.

More than news, I learned network politics and big business intrigue from Sam, who is the best and most gracious mentor anyone could ever have. Ironically, Jimmy Carter seemed to be the only one who was self-conscious about having a black so close. One day in his home town of Plains, Georgia, he was walking the streets, showing us city boys the wonders of the country. With a smirk, he asked me if I had ever seen peanuts growing. After saying no, he took me and the five other journalists assigned to cover his every movement to a house on his family's farm. We met the black man who "took care of this for us. He tended the fields, cooked the meals, stayed in the house for free, and kept some of the profits from the peanuts." I asked if he got to keep a share of the crop, too. Carter said yes. I said, "Does that make him a sharecropper?" His tenant gave me a knowing smile, but Carter missed the humor. He turned cold and never showed me where peanuts came from. For a Southerner who was supposed to be so liberal and comfortable around blacks, Carter was neither. He saw race as a potential problem. The person who was comfortable about race and its politics was Vice President Walter Mondale from Minnesota, where just seeing a black person is a real event.

As time passed, more black reporters and producers were hired at ABC, such as Carole Simpson, who came from NBC, and Bernard Shaw, who came from CBS. Carole is still with ABC, but Bernie left. He had an offer from the fledgling cable network CNN but wanted to stay with ABC. He asked for a raise and a chance to be an anchor. ABC said he had no future as an anchor, so he left and became an anchor for CNN.

In the early 1980s, the women at ABC organized around the lack of numbers, airtime, and visible beats. Carole was their leader. With the help of her husband, who is a computer genius, they presented news management with undeniable evidence that women were second-class citizens at ABC. Roone Arledge, the president of the news division, had a female senior assistant, but women were absent from the other senior positions in News. In fact, none were even on a management track. About the same time, blacks became organized. I was the leader. That was possible because I had become successful, which meant management would at least answer my calls. I had become a featured reporter on the evening news, and, without anyone's help, developed the first medical and health beat on network television. I had to be dealt with; my concerns could not be dismissed. Also, I think management was intrigued with me and wanted to see what else I could do besides medical stories.

Make no mistake, we were all nervous and feared retribution. I had kids about to go to college; I wondered if my ability to pay for their tuition was about to be put in jeopardy. But the representation of blacks at ABC was abysmal. There were only four correspondents, about six producers, and fewer low-level employees. We asked for and received a meeting with senior management. It was to be a lunch in the executive lunch room at ABC's corporate offices in New York. There were nine of us, and it was tense. Word of the lunch spread like wildfire throughout the network. Carole and I were in the New York newsroom, and just before we left, Carole said that a white colleague asked, "What are you going to have for lunch, watermelon?" That person is now a senior manager. Correspondent Ken Walker and I flanked Roone. The senior black producer in the room, Ray Nunn, joked that Ken and I were the *ton ton macout*, what Haitians call the members of the government's hit squad in that country.

We presented our concerns: lack of numbers, airtime, representation in major beats. We were also concerned about how blacks were portrayed and how that portrayal inaccurately stereotyped African-Americans. I complained specifically about the lack of blacks on Brinkley's discussion round-table show. I said its name should be changed to *This Week with Middle-Aged White Men*. We asked for management to hire a person to both oversee making ABC more representative and mentor minorities who were hired. We asked for regular job assessments, so all people could be apprised of their progress or lack there of. We felt ABC should hire a sensitivity specialist to train management and minorities how to better work together. The three-hour session was, at times, tense. As some of the managers became defensive, Roone stepped in and told them to listen, not to react. Still the meeting was going nowhere until the head of finance, Irwin Weiner, rose and challenged his white colleagues, "What we have heard here shows us that we need to act. Don't say we are sensitive, then do nothing. We can choose to do that, but we have to be honest about making that choice and what it means." I have respected Irwin ever since. For awhile, ABC was awash in sensitivity about blacks and women. Professionals led training sessions, a recruiter was hired, more producers and correspondents were hired, we got a little more airtime. We were making progress, but I always had the feeling this was all done grudgingly, and I wondered when the bloom would be off this rose.

For me, and the rest of us, this was our first brush with real corporate power. It was a game we were smart enough to play, but our lack of practice hurt. We knew whatever we received had a price. We were eager to save one of our colleagues who had gotten into trouble, padding expenses. We made a passionate, if thin, argument for a second or maybe third chance. While management was deciding, I was due to go on vacation. A senior manager told me to call from a phone booth on Interstate 95 to get their answer. I did, and our colleague was given another chance. But I was told that a reporter from a newspaper would be calling and would want quotes concerning ABC's new minority advisory board. I was expected to be positive. I was. Why did I do all of this? It was a heady feeling for a time, but I also remembered what Vernon Jordan, the former head of the Urban League and one of Bill Clinton's closest advisers, said once, "Always pay your back, black taxes." He meant always use your success to help those brothers and sisters who haven't made it yet. I had some IOUs built up, so I could spend them. Whites can be generous; blacks must be generous. It is part of the duty of being successful.

Time has passed, and what has happened? There is still no black in senior management. There is no black in a senior position at the flagship broadcast, *World News Tonight*. In the last five years, there has been great turnover in the *World News* senior staff. No black has been hired; I don't know if an African-American has even been interviewed. One producer with a resume and accomplishments as impressive as any was offered a senior job on the weekend news, but he said, "I am ready for the major leagues, why play in the minors?" He was told he was not ready for *World News*, yet a white producer with fewer accomplishments and less seniority was tapped for the *World News* job. After less than a year when that person left, both sides said, "It didn't work out." In fact, now *World News* only has one African-American producer on its rolls. Several describe "being chased off the show," not for racial reasons but for other differences. Several have gone on to great success at other networks. One is now an assistant bureau chief in Washington. *World News* has had one black on the show's inner circle, but he came from outside. He was told after he was hired that he probably wouldn't be there if he were not black. He left after a year.

Race is central to what has happened at ABC, but race does not define the circumstance. In one sense, it is the result of a clash of cultures; not between the races, but between journalism and diversity. ABC, like all journalism outlets, expresses concern about ethnic diversity. But as a recent study at Harvard University noted, "The central press tradition of objectivity is in conflict with the notion that diversity is essential in the newsroom. In an ideal world, good ideas prevail by their own force. In the non-ideal world we inhabit, the implementation of good ideas is as much a problem as their generation."

We journalists cling to the image of objectivity. It is part of how we define ourselves. While other disciplines (history, anthropology, etc.) accept that the nature of a story or event will vary with the personal characteristics, such as social and cultural background of the investigator, journalists resist that notion. Under our tradition, when one's personal history is used to explain a story, that is a defect to be cured, not an inevitability to be accepted. Consequently, the call for diversity may help reporters determine the real nature of what they report, but it is in conflict with the tradition so many journalists hold dear.

That is part of the reason that racial diversity has lagged. Also, the times have changed. Affirmative action programs are as much under fire in journalism as everywhere else in America. In addition, the pool of reporters emerging from journalism schools is not as diverse. Finally, there is no pressure from the outside for newsrooms to diversify. There are no marches, no boycotts, no loud speeches. When I started, there was a push to get blacks ON TV. There has never been an equal push to get us behind the camera where TV is controlled. This is why the diversity bloom is off the rose at ABC. This is why seminars on sensitivity are conducted by people who are not qualified and why there has been no incentive, positive or negative, for managers to diversify their workforce. Recently, there was a directive telling managers that when there is an opening, if it is not filled by a minority, they have to explain why. That is positive, but it is probably too early to look for results.

I am often asked, "What is the most important or interesting story you have ever covered?" That's easy—South Africa. I have been there a number of times both during and after Apartheid. At first, it is odd for an African-American there. I consider myself black, but the black South Africans say I am colored. In that culture, that classification conveys privilege. For me, it hurt that I was seen as someone different from them, and, therefore, not an equal partner in their struggle.

Ironically, being a black American gave me better access to both whites and blacks in South Africa. Whites saw me as an American journalist, someone with whom they needed to curry favor. Blacks saw me as a minority journalist, someone who might be sympathetic to their cause. Most African-Americans look with envy at the peaceful transition to democracy in South Africa. The spirit that attends the remaking of an entire society is uplifting. I imagine it is the same feeling Jefferson and Madison had as they helped create a new America. To report on it was an honor. ABC sent me because I had more knowledge of the situation than other in-house reporters, I had written a 12-page memo outlining a strategy for coverage, and they felt it important to have their senior black correspondent covering this major event. I was assigned a white producer. The one white correspondent who accompanied me was assigned a black producer.

As I said at the beginning, race plays a central role in my career, but I have fought against it defining my career. Part of that is because I believe my talent and hard work are better and more accurate definitions of my success. But that is not to deny race and its importance. If anything, race defines my perception of events that I cover and events that I experience. For whites, I believe the same is true. Many postmodernist scholars say there is no objective reality. Instead, I am part of a growing movement of black intellectuals who subscribe to what is being called the critical race theory. Simply stated, the theory holds that there are competing racial versions of reality that may never be reconciled.

Race affects our perception of reality and our understanding of the world in almost every way. Does the O. J. case make the point? As most blacks, I believed the L.A. police might have planted evidence and lied. Early on, I told ABC that journalistically, race was important in this trial and that they should include black experts as part of their roster of commentators. But the white people who control ABC didn't believe the police would lie, thought the DNA evidence was overwhelming, and were blind to the impact that race might have on those proceedings. No blacks commented on the trial until after the verdict and the outcry—black and white—it caused. Because of the wait, the black commentators were patronized and asked to generalize in ways white commentators were not. ABC had done some polling during the trial that showed the racial division, but the network ignored its own data.

This perceptual gap defines why some stories are deemed important and others are not. For the life of me, I can't understand why the murder of Jon Benet Ramsey, the six-year-old beauty pageant winner, is such an enduring story. We have spent tens of thousands of dollars and devoted hours of airtime to this one murder, yet virtually nothing is mentioned about the murders of black kids who die every day. I think the coverage is racist. My white colleagues say that black kids are killed all the time, but what happened to Jon Benet is unusual, tragic, and, therefore, news. This perceptual gap defines the continuing resistance to diversifying the newsroom. Blacks like me say it is needed because otherwise the *News* can't fairly represent the reality in this country. Whites must believe what is real is what *They* see.

5
The Woman Correspondent
Marlene Sanders

I was there near the beginning. It was 1964 when I became ABC
News's second woman correspondent; Lisa Howard was already on
board. At NBC, there was Pauline Frederick and Nancy Dickerson, and
at CBS, Marya McLaughlin. I do not include Barbara Walters in the mix
since she was an interviewer on *The Today Show* and never a standard
field reporter, which is what we're talking about here. So we were five
among the three networks.

What women have always wanted is to be able to get the assignments and do the job, which sounds simple enough. Today, with the
possible exception of sports, stories are assigned without prejudice in
terms of gender. Women are covering almost everything and that is undeniably progress, but it did not come easy.

My own entry-level job at the network came after nine years of
work in local TV news and radio. I grew up in Cleveland, Ohio, and
inexplicably was passionately interested in politics and social issues beginning in high school. Television was not a factor in my life then. Radio
was where we heard the voices who brought us the news, and those
voices were all male. The phrase "role model" was unknown then, and
for females, there were none. In the mid fifties, I had moved to New
York City in search of a career. At a summer theater where I landed a job
as assistant to the producers, I met Mike Wallace who was about to
begin a television news show in New York. I was hired by his producer,
Ted Yates, to work as a production assistant on *Mike Wallace and
the News* at WABD, New York. There I learned how to put a news
broadcast together, and by the time Mike's breakthrough interview program *Night Beat* came along, I was associate producer. Later, I moved
to coproducer with Mike's successor host, John Wingate, in the interview chair.

I left the station five years later. By then I had produced talk shows,
put together documentaries with acquired footage, and wrote both

news and interview shows. During those last years at channel 5, I met and married Jerry Toobin, and in 1960, our son, Jeff, was born. I had no idea how this mix of motherhood and profession was going to work out, but I was determined that it would. Fortunately for me, my next few years of employment in the industry were New York based. It was only later, at the networks, that travel posed problems that have plagued women in the industry ever since. When Jeff was six months old, I moved to a syndicated late-night talk and entertainment show called *PM East* as a writer/producer, then went to WNEW Radio as a radio documentary producer and broadcaster.

By then nine years had passed, and I was one of the most experienced women around, so I beat the competition in an audition for the job as network correspondent at ABC News. During my nearly fourteen eventful years at ABC, I worked not only as a correspondent but also anchored news and produced documentaries. By the time I left, I was vice president and director of Documentaries, the first female network news vice president in the industry.

But we are interested here in the life of women correspondents, and in a way, I had to invent the job at ABC. After my arrival, the other woman, Lisa Howard, was suspended because of her political activities, so I was alone. As has always been true in this business, one's career rises and falls depending on how one stands with management. Jesse Zousmer, the news v.p. who hired me, knew my background and was interested in my development. He saw to it that I had campaign assignments that got me out of the studio where I had been anchoring a daily five-minute news program. It was a time when women mainly covered soft issues and stories like candidates' wives. We were relegated to the equivalent of a newspaper's woman's page. Few women were running for office, so Pat Nixon, Lady Bird Johnson, and Muriel Humphrey were part of my agenda. However, because ABC News was the upstart third place network and shorthanded, I had plenty of the hard-news assignments as well—everything from mine disasters to the major stories of the 60s.

As Joe Foote has written in his introduction, great stories of the 60s made broadcast correspondents fixtures of American journalism. This was a great time to be in news, not only because of the constant flow of significant stories, but because of the autonomy and confidence the network placed in its correspondents. The constant editing, rewriting, and second guessing by evening news brass that torments today's reporters was minimal. Obviously, there were some editorial changes in footage and copy, but it was usually done in collaboration with the correspondent. No one enjoys being edited, but this was a rational process at work.

When my daily program ended in 1968, I was free to cover more breaking news. Even before then, Zousmer sent me to Vietnam in the spring of 1966, making me the first TV newswoman to report that war, albeit briefly. In the years that followed, I was occupied by reporting on the war's impact on the country, covering protests and counter protests, and following the turmoil at Columbia University and other colleges around the country. During the infamous Democratic convention in Chicago in 1968, I was on hand to cover Eugene McCarthy's campaign. Because they had an exhausting routine, I regularly relieved my male colleagues. As a result, for weeks at a time, I covered most of the presidential candidates. Women then were not assigned the major contenders, and that happily has changed. I was part of the death watch after Bobby Kennedy was assassinated, and was busy into the 70s with hard news.

During all of those early years at ABC, the practice was for correspondents to be their own producers, so I covered the stories with a film crew, then all male. We were all collegial, and I had no problems in being the boss of those units. We only had a producer when the logistics were complicated; for example, on Lady Bird Johnson's five-day whistle stop campaign trip through the South, we had to charter planes to get to affiliate stations, develop and edit the film, and feed the stories to New York. Otherwise, I wrote and produced my own news stories. That system has changed dramatically, causing frustration in the correspondent ranks. Whatever the motive, this diminution of control by the person who actually covered the story has downgraded the role of correspondent to something less than that of trusted reporter.

So far, my story differs little from a male correspondent of the same period, except in the variation of the assignments. But all was not well in the paltry ranks of women at the networks. The civil rights movement had spawned the women's movement, and by the 1970s, it was our turn. We reported on the efforts of women for equality of opportunity in society in general, but we were not part of it. I knew many of the leaders of the women's movement and understood the story, which was then widely misinterpreted by men. Tom Wolf, the director of documentaries at ABC in 1970, recognizing a developing story when he saw it, gave me the go-ahead to do the first documentary on the burgeoning women's movement. It was then visible mostly on college campuses and in the variety of newly formed activist groups. By 1972, I reported on the formation of the National Women's Political Caucus and the increasing number of women running for office. This was women's news of a different variety—the kind I enthusiastically wanted to cover.

Women journalists had finally begun to organize at the Associated Press, the news magazines, and the *New York Times*. Significantly, in 1972, there was a license challenge of ABC's New York affiliate, channel 7, charging blatant sexism. At last, the women at the networks took action. At ABC, we formed the Women's Action Committee; similar groups began at both CBS and NBC. Executive Order 11246, nicknamed Executive Lib, was one of the regulations that seemed to require broadcasters to promote women. Revised Order #4, also known as affirmative action, required nearly all businesses with at least 50 employees and $50,000 in government contracts to reflect the gender balance in their communities. It was this ruling that produced what became known as "the class of '72" at local stations around the country. Many of the top network newswomen were hired at that time, including CBS's Lesley Stahl.

In my book, *Waiting for Prime Time: The Women of Television News*, written with Marcia Rock, we explained in detail how the networks' women's groups worked. At ABC, our meetings with management began with great anxiety as well as exhilaration on our part. (I was by then a documentary producer and correspondent.) Meetings proceeded well, though not without antagonism on both sides. The women of NOW (the National Organization for Women) who filed the license challenge against channel 7 had produced dismal statistics about the lack of women at the station. That made an impression and worked to our benefit. Our efforts were directed at bringing more women into the company at all levels—to increase mobility, wages, and open the doors in the sales area, closed to women until then. Over a period of several years, regular meetings were held, and things began to move.

Our group gradually faded away after the initial gains were made. By the 80s however, it was clear that not enough progress had taken place. Again, the women of ABC organized. Unfortunately, most of the original participants had moved elsewhere, and the new group, now comprised of newswomen only, had no knowledge of our earlier efforts. This was one of the reasons Rock and I wrote our book, so that the wheel would not have to be reinvented each decade. Correspondent Carole Simpson and others confronted management about salary discrepancies they had somehow managed to uncover and complained about what they called institutional sex discrimination. By 1986, some promises had been made, along with actual salary adjustments and some new hires. Since then, slippage has again been noted. But the downsizing of recent years, the increasing number of freelancers hired, and new corporate management has dampened the impulse to organize once again.

Recounting my own experiences at an earlier time makes my career look relatively seamless. That was hardly the case. Some executive producers made my life miserable because of discriminatory assignments. I also had to work out child-care arrangements at home so that my sporadic, unscheduled travel assignments could be accommodated. Because of good household help and a supportive husband, I was able to accomplish this without major problems, but at that time, I knew of no other women in the same boat. My major struggles took place at work, while my home life progressed without much anxiety on my or my husband's part.

The problem of travel and long hours has been one difficulty shared unequally by men and women in the business. It is simply a fact of life that women have the major responsibility for their children. It is also true that dogged ambition is a component of the job, and for most in this profession, the work is forced to come, if not first, close to it. As a result, many women have opted out of network jobs and have gone to local stations where travel, at least, is not an issue. Job sharing has been almost unknown, except for two such arrangements at NBC. Two women correspondents, Lisa Rudolph and Victoria Corderi, also share. They report for the magazine show *Dateline* and believe that this way their family life does not suffer since they have more time with their children. In my opinion, this is not the route to network stardom or to the ranks of the A list. We also do not know if the women will return to full-time work. Job sharing may, however, provide a more balanced life. Magazine shows involve travel, but it is scheduled in advance. Most women at the networks are B-list correspondents anyway, relegated to early morning broadcasts, weekends, and assigned peripheral stories. Stardom for the few women who achieve it is now on the magazine shows, not on the nightly news.

Along with the growing star system in the ranks of correspondents, other factors have made the work less rewarding and more difficult for women. Those of us who were there early got older! Alas, beauty fades. The weather-beaten male who resembles the statesmen we know and respect is now more than ever the voice and face of authority on the tube. While he has lines of character etched into his face, we have lines, period. The standard for women is simply different. Looks count in America, and looks count on the TV screen as well as in the movies. While there is not exactly panic in the ranks, the coffers of plastic surgeons have surely benefited. We don't want to lose our jobs because of age and will do all we can to keep them.

The demands of the job have produced a corps of female producers and correspondents largely made up of either unmarried women or women without children. Few with families have managed more than one child. For some who have neither husbands nor children, this is a willing compromise or perhaps just the result of a demanding, nomadic profession. But when the jobs end, as they inevitably do, there may be memories of important stories and an interesting life, but one without lovers, husbands, or children. I, for one, wanted it all and pretty much had it. Not everyone has been so lucky. The newer generation of men in the business who hold almost all of the top managerial jobs may be more amenable to compromises in schedules that make family life more possible. But the competitive nature of the business and the way news breaks may be obstacles that are simply too great.

Another thorn in the side of correspondents has been the hiring of celebrities or outside experts untrained in the business. What chance does a woman who is a mere journalist have when the FOX network hires a former judge like Catherine Crier, or CBS brings in New York Congresswoman Susan Molinari as a weekend anchor?

Several other factors have changed the nature of the business affecting how women do their jobs. The 1997 survey, the 10th annual "Women, Men, and Media" report tells an interesting story. Media specialist Andrew Tyndall who did the research based on 1996 figures says that while the networks are focusing more on domestic issues, such as education, families, health and race relations, more and more men are being assigned to those stories.

While men are moving into beats where women used to predominate, women have not covered more of the mostly male preserves of crime, terrorism, and the military. It was a hard-won struggle to get conservative, overly protective senior management to let us cover war and urban violence. After winning major struggles on that issue, we can now cover the hard foreign beats, wars, and revolution. Ironically, the U.S. appetite for foreign news has declined. The Cold War is over, and media are looking less and less at the outside world. Feminist Betty Friedan views the less-macho reporting roles of men as a sign of progress, but it doesn't seem to work both ways. It's not that we feel we have to prove ourselves equal to the task of covering danger, but frequently those stories of international turmoil are the big ones, and we want to be there. Today we are finally there, but those stories just don't often make the main news broadcasts!

Other interesting facts from the study include:

- In 1996, the networks assigned approximately 20 percent of all reports on their nightly newscasts to women, up from 14 percent in 1988.

- Nineteen percent of all stories were filed and aired by women.

- Women in the D.C. bureaus got the most airtime.

- Story topics women covered were mostly arts, media, entertainment, sex and family, and federal elections.

- The coverage of health and medicine stories filed by women declined from 32 percent in 1988 to 12 percent in 1996, making it one of the two beats (the other being environment) on which women became less prominent.

Has the long struggle, which officially began in the 70s, produced the results we wanted? We wanted more women in news, and that began to happen slowly—a few news writers, a producer here or there, a few women on the assignment desk, and the battle with the unions to bring women in as members of technical jobs. Women producers now cover crime and war zones.

Figures are hard to come by beyond the faces you see on the screen. There are many more women field producers, as well as executive producers of major news broadcasts and magazine shows. Women are now shooting and editing the stories as well.

To sum up, there is a two-tier level, not only of correspondents, but of job satisfaction. For both men and women on the A list, there are the rewards of airtime and good money. For the B-list players, the grunts in the field, the victims of the big-foot anchors or star correspondents, there is grumbling and paranoia.

Our hope is that the standards of journalism we believe in will be upheld and not debased. No matter what indignities we suffer at the hands of our employers or the dangers we subject ourselves to in the field, it is a fascinating and rewarding life.

6

Clinton 1992: Behind the Scenes with the Political Correspondent

Chris Bury

The most intense year of my career at ABC News began, strangely enough, in Mort's Deli under the elevated tracks in Chicago's Loop. I had been interviewing Mort, the portly and bearded proprietor, for what was to be a wry look at the national pickle shortage gripping America's delicatessens in the winter of 1992. This story was supposed to have been a show-ender, one of the light-hearted pieces that networks often use to close their evening news broadcasts. I was then based in Chicago, assigned to the Midwest bureau as a general assignment correspondent, covering news from Minneapolis to Memphis; floods to farming; politics to pickles. During the interview with Mort, my beeper vibrated on my belt several times. As soon as the interview was completed, I thanked Mort and called the New York assignment desk. Mimi Gurbst, the national assignment editor, told me to hook up with the Clinton campaign that night in Atlanta. "How long will I be gone?" I asked. "Probably just over a week," Mimi replied, "until the Super Tuesday primaries." I had just enough time to run home to Evanston, pack a bag, kiss my wife and two young sons good-bye, and grab a taxicab to O'Hare airport for the flight to Atlanta. It was March 1, 1992. I would not return, except for rare days off, until November 7, four days after Bill Clinton had been elected president of the United States.

My former colleague at ABC News, Jeff Greenfield, likes to say the relationship between politicians and the media is like two people who have sex after meeting for the first time at a bar. They use each other, there is no emotional attachment, but both participants get something out of it. In a national campaign for president, the candidates, their staffs, and the media travel together by plane and by bus, cocooned together in something campaigns call "the bubble." It's a strange little world, where the country speeds by in a blur of staged events. The ethic, for the campaign, is to manipulate the media. The ethic, for the reporters, is to be too savvy and cynical not to point out every last manipulation. It is a kind of ritual Kabuki dance. The candidate gets his message out; we get our stories. It's an adversarial and symbiotic relationship. We often don't like each other, but we do need each other.

In the early 1992, after Clinton pulled ahead of the pack, New York headquarters decided to put full campaign teams on both candidates. That meant each campaign would be assigned an on-air correspondent, field producer, and camera crew, in addition to the off-air reporter. The night of March 1, 1992, Lee Kamlet, a veteran ABC News field producer, and I hooked up with the Clinton campaign in Atlanta. As producer, Kamlet's job was to supervise the camera crew, keep track of videotape, arrange all logistics, supervise the tape-editing process, confer with the assignment desk and various broadcasts (*World News Tonight, Good Morning America, Nightline, World News Now,* the weekend news shows, etc.), and produce a crisply edited, network-quality broadcast piece. As correspondent, my job was to make sense of the candidate's day, develop a theme, keep track of what the opposing candidates were doing and saying, confer constantly with the broadcast show producers in New York, write a script, get it approved by the senior broadcast producers and anchors, record my narration, shoot on-camera stand-ups, and get it all done in time for producer Kamlet to cut the piece with a videotape editor and feed it to New York for that night's broadcast. No matter the logistical complications, candidate's schedule, or technical problems, the feed to New York was never to be missed. At *World News Tonight,* a producer and correspondent might be forgiven one missed feed during a campaign. But those of us in the field knew a reputation for frequently missing feeds could jeopardize careers of correspondents and producers.

The Pack

In Iowa and New Hampshire, the early primaries, the media follow candidates around in small charter planes, commercial flights, and rented cars. Once a candidate becomes a front-runner and the campaign takes on a more hectic schedule, the media and candidate travel everywhere together via chartered jet. The media actually pay most of the cost, since campaigns traditionally charge news organizations at least one and a half times first-class airfare for the privilege of traveling with the candidate. Since only the biggest news organizations can afford this kind of coverage, the permanent traveling pack consists of the major television networks (ABC, CBS, NBC, CNN), big national newspapers *(New York Times, Washington Post, Wall Street Journal, USA Today)*, major regional papers *(Los Angeles Times, Chicago Tribune, Boston Globe, New York Newsday, New York Post, New York Daily News, Dallas Morning News, Houston Chronicle)*, wire services (Associated Press, Reuters, United Press International), newspaper syndicates (Copley News Service, Gannett, Cox), weekly news magazines *(Newsweek, Time, U.S. News and World Report)*, and radio networks (National Public Radio, CBS, ABC, Mutual Broadcasting). Local media, international journalists, and specialty news outlets (MTV, *People, New Republic)* join the pack for a few days at a time. So do "big-foot" columnists, such as David Broder, Robert Evans, and Jack Germond, who spend a few days with the campaign to gather grist for a column or two.

The job of the permanent press pack is to find the news in what a candidate does or says. Since most members of this pack memorize a candidate's stock speech within a few days, the challenge is to be keenly aware of the campaign's nuances and use them to develop stories. As Timothy Crouse discovered in his landmark chronicle of campaign coverage, *The Boys on the Bus,* the dynamics of the press pack often produce a weary "sameness" to the coverage. Reporters incessantly ask each other, "What's your lead?" meaning "What angle of the campaign are you going to write about today?" Because editors at the networks and big newspapers are constantly reading wire service reports back at their desks, reporters on the campaign are often loathe to develop leads that are different from the wire stories. They know their editors will be asking, "Why didn't you have that AP story?" or "You know, the wires are leading with such and such." The *New York Times* and *Washington Post* are also read by virtually every top political editor and, as a result, are among the most powerful influences on setting the agenda for campaign coverage. That may help explain why the network news reports and big national papers so frequently seem to have nearly identical leads on a candidate's day.

In 1992 during the New Hampshire primary, the national media became obsessed with the story of Bill Clinton's conflicting accounts of manipulating his draft status during the Vietnam War. This was an important and explosive story, of course. But in New Hampshire, reporters spent so much time hounding Clinton on the draft question that they ignored his campaign message and the response it was getting among voters. At campaign events, voters were asking about health care, military preparedness, and education. And yet the press pack, weary of Clinton's stock answers on such subjects, asked only about his avoidance of the draft. To me, this itself was a story and a good way to differentiate my coverage from the pack's. So I gathered material from several campaign events around New Hampshire and contrasted voters concerns with press questions in this February 14, 1992, report for ABC's *World News Tonight with Peter Jennings*:

BURY: In Portsmouth the other day, a voter confronted Bill Clinton about defending his country.

(Voter): "And I think we're just cutting back a little too fast and a little too much."

BURY: Clearly, the question concerned the defense budget in 1992, not Clinton's dealings with the draft in 1969.

(Clinton speech excerpt): "We now have a defense budget that is organized to defend against the Soviet threat that doesn't exist any more."

BURY: In the campaign's final crunch, questions of Clinton's character, his personal life, and the draft are pursued daily, almost always by the press.

(Reporter's question): "What about the fact that people keep raising these questions?"

(Clinton): "People don't. People don't."

BURY: And that is the trouble for Clinton. The press hounds him about his character. Voters seem more worried about other things, like the woman in Nashua today who broke down telling Clinton that the cost of medicine was swallowing her savings. And the voters who listened at Dartmouth last night, where Clinton talked about health care reform, a middle-class tax cut, and spending more on education.

(Clinton speech): "What you have to decide is do I have the best vision? Do I have the best plan? Do I have the best record? Who can best change this country?"

BURY: Many who heard him were aware of the character questions.

(Woman voter): "Prior to hearing him, I was very concerned about them, and I think I would not have voted for him. After hearing him, I think he expressed in very concrete terms how he cares for people."

(Man voter): "His character has been in such a test the last couple of weeks that he didn't let that dominate tonight at all. That wasn't the issue in this; the issues were."

BURY: Some people do care about issues such as Clinton's attempts to avoid military service in Vietnam. At a high school in Tilton, some of New Hampshire's youngest voters said it bothered them.

(Boy): "If you're against the war, that's fine; you can protest or

whatever. But when your country calls on you to serve for it,
I think you should serve your country."

BURY: But after a Clinton speech to retirees, no one we talked to
cared.

(Man): "I'm a World War II veteran. I didn't put much credence
to it at all. I really don't feel it's an issue."

BURY: Still, the difficulty for Clinton in the next few days is to
deliver a message on his terms, not the messenger's. Chris
Bury, ABC News, Manchester, New Hampshire.

The idea behind this piece, broadcast a few days before the New
Hampshire primary, was to show that voters and the press pack had
quite different interests. By focusing so exclusively on Clinton's draft
problems, the press was missing an equally important story—many voters didn't care much about Clinton's draft evasion, and they were hungry
to hear him speak about the things that mattered to them: health care,
taxes, and education. Was this piece too soft on Clinton? By now, the
draft charges had been well reported, and I felt this other story—Clinton's
strong personal performance among voters—had been receiving almost
no attention. Sometimes the hardest thing for a campaign reporter to do
is break away from the pack and its safe, conventional coverage. But it is
also the only way to set your reporting apart from the rest.

The Pace

For a network correspondent or any reporter covering a national campaign, some of the most challenging demands are logistical and physical.
In 1992, not only did producer Lee Kamlet and I have to cover Clinton
full time, we had to catch up with him all the time, too. Nearly every
day, Kamlet and I would have to break-off from the campaign in mid-
afternoon to prepare our report for that night's *World News Tonight*.
This involved finding a taxicab in some strange city, hustling to the near-
est ABC-affiliated television station, finding phones, fax machines, and
an ABC News videotape editor, who would have lugged 16 cases of edit
gear from the airport that morning. Sometimes we would not have time
to reach an ABC affiliate and would edit our pieces from airport han-
gars, hotel rooms, and convention halls. During my first campaign,
covering Gary Hart in 1984, most campaign reporters still banged out
their stories on portable typewriters. By 1992, typewriters had vanished,
replaced by laptop computers. Kamlet would carefully log every Clinton
speech, press conference, and campaign event into his computer, noting
the exact time of each. Our camera crews would record time of day
codes on the videotape. This system allowed us to edit our pieces with

maximum speed. The tape editors could quickly locate the sound bites and pictures we needed by matching Kamlet's log time with the time codes on videotape. The time pressures were very real because Kamlet and I often would not reach the ABC affiliate or other edit point until late in the afternoon. On most days, we had no more than two or three hours to write a script, get it approved by *World News Tonight* senior producers, edit the tape, and transmit the piece, via satellite, to New York. Team effort is a well-worn cliché, but in network news, it is absolutely essential. The correspondent, field producer, photographer, sound technician, videotape editor and senior producers at headquarters must all perform under pressure. For a correspondent, writing fast is nearly as important as writing well. The evening broadcast deadline, 6:30 P.M. Eastern, is set in stone. Legendary press critic A. J. Liebling captured the swagger and insecurity of reporters under deadline in his famous boast, "I can write faster than anyone who can write better. And I can write better than anyone who can write faster."

In these late afternoon editing sessions, I would often envy my colleagues in the print press. They could simply write their stories in their laptops and feed them over telephone lines to their newspapers and magazines. A good network television report must weave picture, sound, and writing into a cohesive piece. In March 1992, I tried to use these tools to show Clinton's iron constitution on the campaign trail. The piece begins with a scene from a Clinton campaign event of a local band playing the Buddy Holly classic, "Rock Around the Clock."

(Music Up: "We're gonna rock around the clock tonight. . . .")
BURY: It could be the Clinton campaign song. Expectations for
    him in the South are high. To meet them, Clinton has given
    new meaning to the words "brutal pace."
(Montage of sound clips from Clinton in three separate cities):
    "If you look at how the crime issue has convulsed the city of
    Houston . . ."; "I want to thank my friends and neighbors in
    Tennessee. . . ."; "Florida's got an unemployment rate of over
    eight and a half percent."
(Narration over map showing 21 cities that Clinton has visited)
BURY: Since he left Georgia six days ago, Clinton has flown to
    21 cities in Florida, South Carolina, Arkansas, Texas, Ten-
    nessee, Louisiana, and Missouri—8,966 miles.
(Interview with Clinton): "It never ends. There's always another
    set of challenges as soon as you get off. I haven't had a day
    off in a good while."
BURY: Yesterday, Clinton got up at dawn in Houston and wound

up at two this morning in Orlando. Reporters call him, "Robo-candidate." Wounded by questions about his integrity, he keeps going and going and never stops talking. . . . talking policy at baseball games . . .

(Picture of Clinton talking at ball game. Sound up): "We need a new energy policy."

BURY: As he eats, and it seems, when he sleeps. (Pictures of Clinton talking while eating, picture of a very tired-looking candidate)

BURY: For Clinton, the campaign grind does not seem a chore. He cannot resist the temptation of one last handshake. Even for a seasoned politician like Bill Clinton, all the miles and hours and crises of his campaign have led to some personal wear and tear. Since New Hampshire, Clinton has suffered from a chronic cough.

(Sound up): "Thank you so much. Whoa, I'm hoarse." (Picture of Clinton getting off plane at 2:00 A.M., looking whipped)

BURY: Late in the day, his voice often goes, and the campaign smile fades. He knows fatigue can be dangerous in politics.

(Clinton interview): "I think almost every major mistake I've ever made in public life and some in private life, I've made because I was just so tired I didn't know what I was doing."

(Picture of Clinton jogging) BURY: On the eve of Super Tuesday, Clinton is tired. But he keeps up the pace, aware the primaries are as much an endurance test as a political one. Chris Bury, ABC News, Miami.

In this piece, the music, pictures, map, interview, speech excerpts, and script all attempt to support the story line of a candidate who is working tremendously hard and paying a personal price. The segment runs 1 minute, 50 seconds. Since time is so precious, all elements must pull their weight in helping to tell the story. After feeding our *World News Tonight* piece to New York, Kamlet and I usually had to produce a second, shorter piece for the next day's *Good Morning America*. Then, I wrote and recorded several pieces for ABC News Radio. Finally, I would record an on-camera "debrief" of the day's events for the overnight news show, *World News Now.* This would be a minute-long piece, directly to camera, where I would highlight the top two or three news elements of the day. After finishing our reports for all the various broadcasts, Kamlet and I would head back to the airport and fly to whatever city the Clinton campaign had ended in that day so we could be on hand to do it all over again the next morning.

Competition

For network correspondents, the political world changed dramatically in 1992. In the 1984 campaign, the three major networks were really the only game in town for candidates who needed to get their message across on television. CNN was still a fledgling competitor. By 1992, CNN had grown up into a first-rate news network with a serious commitment to political coverage. The number of television news organizations interested in campaign coverage seemed to grow exponentially. MTV (cable music television) even had its own correspondent, Tabitha Soren, who occasionally joined the Clinton press pack. Other outlets, such as talk radio, were growing as forums for political coverage. In 1992, I not only had to worry about my standard competitors, but also my colleagues in newly developing media. The Clinton campaign attempted to take full advantage of this changing media scene. Because candidates like to deliver their messages on their terms, without the skeptical filter of network and newspaper reporting, the Clinton campaign reached out to other media whenever it could. During the New York primary campaign, for example, Clinton had been teased mercilessly by radio personality Don Imus, who routinely described the candidate as "Bubba" and "that Arkansas hillbilly." Clinton was also getting a hard time from the notorious New York City tabloids, which had focused on his draft and marital problems to the exclusion of almost everything else. So the campaign decided Clinton should appear on the Imus show to demonstrate his own humor and even toughness in the face of adversity. How does a mainstream network correspondent deal with a candidate's attempt to bypass traditional media? By doing a story on it, of course! Here's how I tried to show Clinton's attempt to soften his image in the hard-boiled New York City media market:

BURY: Governor Clinton was ready to play along this morning when he called in to Don Imus, a popular and very aggressive New York radio personality who has regularly referred to him as "Bubba."
(Governor Clinton): "Good morning, Don."
(Imus): "How are you?"
(Governor Clinton): "I'm all right. I'm disappointed you didn't call me 'Bubba.' That's an honorable term where I come from. It's just southern for 'mensch.'"
BURY: "Mensch," as New Yorkers know, is Yiddish for "good person," "regular guy"—just the image Clinton tried to get across as he made fun of himself on the radio; Clinton's way to punch through the bad press he's gotten in New York.
(Imus): "So, how are you? Do you want to go back to Arkansas?

It's like you've been mugged here in New York, isn't it?"
(Governor Clinton): "Well, I'm having a good time, you know. I'm trying to mug back."

BURY: (with pictures of Clinton surrounded by New York media pack): Just three days ago, Clinton complained of being a media punching bag. Since then, he's been told about the best way to avoid a mugging.

(Paul Begala [Clinton adviser]): "The only people who get mugged in New York are the people who look scared. And I just thought that was the best advice."

BURY: So today, Clinton took that advice and hit the streets of New York. First stop, Brooklyn, for the kind of hand-to-hand campaigning Clinton likes, and his staff likes to see on TV, then on to the Lion's Den: Wall Street, which Clinton has often criticized as a symbol of greed. In an elaborately staged rally, flanked by flags and supporters, Clinton stuck to his guns.

(Clinton): "The stock market tripled while wages went down, the work week lengthened, unemployment went up. That's what happened, and it's not right."

BURY: For Clinton, it was a day of back to the basics: babies and autographs. His campaign, looking wounded just days ago, now proclaims—but cannot prove—that Clinton has turned the corner here. That after a frosty welcome, New York is warming to Clinton, and he to it. Chris Bury, ABC News, New York.

In this report, I was attempting to demonstrate how Clinton had reached out in a different medium, talk radio, to confront his critics and improve his image in the nation's toughest media market. The strategy worked. Clinton went on to score a decisive victory over Jerry Brown in the New York primary.

The Clinton campaign reached out to nontraditional political media in other strategic ways. In June 1992, after Governor Clinton had clinched the Democratic nomination, the phenomenon of Ross Perot had pushed Clinton off the network newscasts. Frankly, not much was happening in the Clinton campaign, and Perot was a fresher story. At this point, the campaign was eager to generate some national attention for Clinton, differentiate Clinton from Ross Perot, and reach out to younger viewers. So Clinton appeared on the *Arsenio Hall Show* that had a younger, hipper audience than the nightly network news broadcasts. And, in a rare public display, Clinton played the saxophone wearing sunglasses. For the campaign, it was a double public relations coup:

Clinton got a free ride on the *Arsenio Hall Show*, and the network news broadcasts all noticed. This was my report:

> BURY: There he was, Clinton as Elvis, belting out "Heartbreak Hotel" on the *Arsenio Hall Show*, the new, cool candidate on display.
>
> *(Arsenio Hall):* "It's good to see a Democrat blowing something other than an election."
>
> BURY: To avoid blowing this one, Clinton's advisers know they must get voters to give their man another look. Last night's appearance was a way for Clinton to show off the personality behind the politician.
>
> *(Arsenio Hall):* "What do you like, the old Elvis, or which stamp? You know, I know you're an Elvis fan."
>
> *(Clinton):* "I led a national crusade for the young Elvis."
>
> *(Arsenio Hall):* "Really?"
>
> *(Clinton):* "Yeah, you know, when you get old, I mean, he got fat like me."
>
> BURY: The idea is to show Clinton, though serious about issues, does not take himself too seriously. Last night, he explained his infamous remark about never inhaling marijuana.
>
> *(Clinton):* "I wasn't trying to get a good conduct medal for saying I didn't inhale. I was just nervously pointing out that it was another of those things I tried to do and failed at in life."
>
> BURY: The different approach to the media by Clinton has a lot to do with the media success of Ross Perot. Even as Clinton clinched the nomination, he has all but disappeared from the media radar screen, except when reporters would ask Clinton about Perot. That so frustrated his aides they limited news media access to Clinton and looked for friendlier outlets.
>
> *(Paul Begala [Clinton adviser]):* "And we just can't sit back and expect people just to sort of get our story from the wind. They need to learn it. We need to tell them about it, and we're willing to try unconventional, different things to do it."
>
> BURY: Even if that means more music with the message. Clinton knows that before voters will hear him out as a politician, they must first get more comfortable with him as a person. Chris Bury, ABC News, San Antonio.

Our job, as network correspondents, was to show how the candidate was using the new media, and why. But the proliferation of new outlets did not change our basic job: to cover the candidate's every move, report on nuances in his message, and point out conflicts or discrepancies when they arose. In the 1996 presidential election, all candidates had home pages on the Internet, where cyber-surfing voters can find out campaign positions and candidate profiles. This is certainly a positive development, and the more information available for voters, the better. But candidates are so adept at manipulating their messages, on their own terms, that network correspondents, like newspaper reporters, can serve as a useful and important check on campaign puffery and misleading rhetoric.

Spin

For a network correspondent covering a national campaign, nothing is more exhausting than the perpetual spin of campaign advisers, consultants, and pollsters. Spin is a campaign's way of portraying all news events in the best favorable light for the candidate. In the Clinton campaign, the spin doctors (campaign advisers) included consultants Paul Begala and James Carville, press secretary Dee Dee Myers, and communications director George Stephanopoulos. Such advisers present a dilemma for reporters because they tend to be the best sources on a campaign. Yet everything they tell you must be filtered through a reporter's healthy skepticism because their overriding interest is the candidate's success.

In covering the first presidential debate at Washington University in St. Louis, I was wired to appear live with Peter Jennings immediately after the debate was over. Even before the debate had ended, George Stephanopoulos made a bee-line for my camera position, to give me his take on how well Clinton had performed. Dozens of camera crews had trailed him. I was thoroughly embarrassed as Stephanopoulos, surrounded by cameras, sought me out to say, "It's all over. Clinton will be the next president." The statement was bald puffery, of course, yet the Clinton campaign was hardly alone in its spinning. President Bush's campaign team had actually given its operatives a map of the press area at Washington University designating where its senior spinners and mere spinners should fan out after the debate. My former colleague, White House correspondent Brit Hume, likes to say that a spin doctor can only be believed if he says his own candidate has failed. Needless to say, that has never happened to me.

Some of the most outrageous spin from the campaign staff came during the Clinton-Gore bus tours, which had been so successful in promoting the new Democratic ticket after the national convention in New York. In addition to the scheduled campaign events and rallies, the bus caravans would pull off at "unscheduled" stops, where campaign advisers assured us "spontaneous" demonstrations of support had magically gathered by the side of the road. It took only a few interviews, of course, to discover that the events had been purposefully left off the schedule and, in fact, had been meticulously organized to appear spontaneous. If the campaign had trouble spinning network correspondents, it could go directly to the local stations. The Clinton campaign lined up dozens of satellite interviews with local anchors, who could usually be counted on to ask softer questions than the network reporters. The campaign also offered to help local stations produce town meetings, a low-cost way for Clinton to get his message out unfiltered by network correspondents. On the bus tours, the campaign arranged for anchors from small stations, who could never afford the price of a seat on the press charter, to ride with the candidate and get unusual access. The campaign's mission was to get the candidate on the air in 75 markets every day in addition to the network news.

The Clinton spin operation was particularly attuned for political counterattack. At Little Rock headquarters, campaign consultant James Carville ran the war room, a headquarters for opposition research. Carville's mission was to respond to any attacks on Clinton within the day's news cycle, so no accusation would go unanswered on the evening news. Sometimes Clinton responded to charges before those of us covering him had even heard them, as I tried to point out in this story:

BURY: For the third time in less than a week, Governor Clinton interrupted a scheduled day-off to summon reporters to the Governor's mansion to hear his response to Republican attacks. The Bush campaign is making him the issue, Clinton argues, because it lacks a specific agenda.

(Clinton): "If you don't have a record to run on, you don't have a vision to offer the American people, and you desperately, desperately, desperately want to stay in power, what else do you have to do?"

BURY: As for Sunday's Bush campaign release that ridiculed everything from Clinton's eating habits to rumors of his infidelity, Clinton claimed not to be bothered.

(Clinton): "I can't afford to be preoccupied by that sort of nickel-and-dime stuff. I am far more upset by the comments that the president made about health care."

BURY: Yesterday, within minutes after the president said Clinton's health care policy would lead to a system with the compassion of the KGB, Clinton was already defending it, even before most reporters knew about Bush's attack.

(Clinton): "You haven't asked me about this, but as I understand it, the Bush campaign put out a statement today. . . ."

BURY: Since last week, when the Bush campaign began daily attacks on issues from taxes to welfare, the Clinton camp has fired back each time. At the first hint of Republican criticism, a rapid response team gears up. Their mission: to get Clinton's side of the story on the evening news.

(James Carville): "I mean Barney Fife said it one time: there's only two kinds, the quick and the dead. In this business, it's the same thing. We miss a news cycle, and we're gone."

BURY: The danger is no matter how quickly Clinton responds, it is a day not spent defining the campaign on his terms. Chris Bury, ABC News, Little Rock.

Limitations

Covering a candidate from the campaign trail is like covering a baseball game when you can only see the shortstop. The dynamics of a presidential campaign are so complex and varied that even network correspondents traveling full time with the candidate get only a partial view. We cannot see what's going on at headquarters, the policy and issues debates, the fund-raising operations, and behind-the-scenes maneuvering. Consequently, we miss some good stories. Network news is frequently criticized for spending too much time on campaign conflict and not enough time on issues. Some of that criticism is valid, but network correspondents covering a candidate's daily trials and tribulations simply do not have time to prepare exhaustive pieces on every important issue. To address that shortcoming, in 1992, ABC News pioneered a two-level approach to campaign reporting. ABC News beat-reporters in national security, education, the environment, social welfare, law, and medicine tracked and reported major campaign issues for the longer "American Agenda" segment on *World News Tonight*. Those of us on the campaign trail handled issues as they came up on a daily or "spot news" basis. In these reports from the trail, issues are always framed in a political context. Here is a typical daily issue report, on education, from a Clinton campaign swing in California:

BURY: The Clinton campaign built a Hollywood backdrop for its big push on education reforms. In a theme he plans to pound until November, Clinton ridiculed George Bush's promise four years ago to be "the education president."

(Clinton): "America needs an education president who shows up for class every day, not just every four years."

BURY: Clinton promised, in his first 100 days as president, to send Congress an ambitious plan to improve schools. It includes national standards and testing for teachers and students, guaranteed access to preschool through Head Start,

federal loans for anyone who wants to attend college, and a
national apprenticeship program for those who do not.
Clinton would give families a choice among public schools,
but unlike Bush . . .

(Clinton): "I am unalterably opposed to a voucher system to
give people public money to take to private schools."

BURY: Clinton's ideas for reforming education are more specific
than his plans to pay for them. He says it is a question of
priorities.

(Clinton): "Surely a country that found 500 billion dollars to
bail out the savings and loan industry can find 5 billion dollars to fund the Head Start program."

BURY: In Arkansas, Clinton raised sales taxes to spend more on
schools. He required competency tests for teachers; beefed
up the curriculum in math, science, and languages; and re-
voked driver's licenses of high school dropouts. For all his
attempts to improve education in a poor state, Clinton knows
he is also vulnerable. Arkansas still scrapes the bottom of
many national rankings that measure the quality of education. And the Bush campaign is certain to point that out.
Chris Bury, ABC News, Los Angeles.

This was a "quickie" issues report from the field. Yet, it did manage
to summarize the candidate's position on education, point out potential
problems (vagueness on financing), and recap Clinton's record, good
and bad, in Arkansas. The networks performed better on policy issues
than we did on complicated, investigative stories, such as the Whitewater
scandal. When this story broke in the *New York Times*, most reporters,
including me, were far too accepting of the Clintons' response that they
had lost money on the investment, and, therefore, it was no big deal.
This is not a story we could have explored very well from the campaign
trail, but we should have pushed our news organizations to launch independent investigative efforts of our own.

Closing Thought

In the waning days of the Clinton campaign, the crowds were getting
larger and larger, and the candidate and his campaign staff were growing ever more confident. Nonetheless, Clinton decided to end the
campaign running like the underdog. In the last 48 hours of the campaign, Clinton held nine rallies in eight states, covering 2,000 miles in
the final day. By the time Peter Jennings tossed a question to me live on
Election Night, I had not slept for nearly three days. I have no recollec-

tion of what I said or whether it made any sense at all. Since my beeper had buzzed in Mort's Deli eight months before, I had traveled tens of thousands of miles, produced hundreds of stories for various ABC News broadcasts, and seen democracy at work up close. I was tired and anxious to return to a normal life with my family, but the campaign year had been exhilarating, too. In an election year, the presidential campaign is THE story. And for a political reporter, the only thing more difficult than covering the campaign . . . is not covering it.

Political journalists are under increasing criticism for contributing to the coarseness of our civic life. And, no doubt, campaign reporters often do emphasize conflict over substantive reporting on critical issues. Yes, we are, at times, preoccupied with the mechanics: polls, strategy, and tactics. Yet some of this criticism seems naive. Political campaigns, by their very nature, are filled with conflict. Campaigns, after all, are contests; struggles of ideas, personalities, and organizations. The object is to win, at almost all costs. Candidates rely on negative commercials because experience has taught them negative ads often resonate with voters in a way positive commercials do not. If one candidate attacks another in a commercial or on the campaign trail, it is our job as reporters to inform the voters. Journalists report on polls, tactics, and strategy because they are a critical part of modern campaigns. We cannot pretend that presidential campaigns are waged as pristine forums on policy. That would be a great disservice to the public, because it simply is not an accurate reflection. Our job is to report what presidential campaigns are, not what some critics think they ought to be.

7

The Best of Times . . .

Jim Bittermann

No dinner gathering of network foreign correspondents—and there are fewer and fewer these days—is ever complete until someone among the TV types stares nostalgically into the dregs of his wine glass and says mournfully, "Well, I guess we saw the best of it." At which point, the others around the table all nod in somber agreement, and the mood starts to take a nosedive until someone lightens the atmosphere by retelling for the 500th time the story about the parrot in the bar at the Commodore Hotel in Beirut that could mimic the sound of incoming artillery; or the time the ABC and NBC producers had to join forces to kick down a door at Algerian Television in order to get a satellite transmission on the air; or any number of other crazy, unfortunate, or silly memories of what once was done in the unholy pursuit of foreign news. The old-war stories can improve the mood around the dinner table, but they cannot mask a central truth—that in network foreign news coverage the best times are behind us.

Anyone overseas and covering news for a network between the late 1970s and mid 1980s was a part of it. During the better part of a decade, international news coverage at ABC, CBS, and NBC went through a period of unprecedented growth, keen competition, ever greater technical capability, unending curiosity from the editors back home, and bottomless bank accounts. In short, it was one hell of a good time. It was driven by any number of factors: the Cold War had taken a dramatic turn, terrorism was expanding across borders, the networks were making money and growing at an exponential rate, and it became technically easier to gather news farther and farther afield.

From my perspective, the business of television reporting from abroad changed forever one Sunday night in August 1978—one month after I arrived. I had yet to even find an apartment in Rome and was still living in the Eden Hotel just off the Via Veneto. This was ancient Rome— I mean Rome before beepers and cellular telephones—so how could I know until I arrived back from a leisurely Italian meal that NBC had been desperately searching for me? Pope Paul VI had been stricken at his summer home in Castel Gondolfo, about 40 miles from the city. He could die at any time. Like anyone at such a moment, I prayed a silent prayer for his recovery—not entirely out of Christian charity, but because, having just arrived in town, I had no idea what to do if the pope were to die. What is more, having been raised a Protestant in a Protestant town in the largely Protestant Midwest, I had barely a clue about the workings of the Vatican or the Catholic Church.

But the pope simply would not live, and suddenly I felt like I was going to die. Because as I rushed over to Italian television, skimming through the wire copy and trying to get my thoughts in order, I realized that I, the new kid, was about to go on the air against two network legends, Winston Burdett and Bert Quint, both of whom had reported on the Vatican for years. I can still remember Burdett sitting in the Italian television studio, flawlessly ad-libbing the first report on the pope's death in his slow melancholy tones, "And soon, perhaps this very night, the attendants to the Holy Father will remove the sacred ring from his finger, a symbol of shifting power, a symbol that soon there will be a new leader of the world's 600 million Catholics." He made it sound so weighty. The ring removal was news to me, and there was no time to double-check that figure on the number of Catholics. I was only barely able to get on and off the air without embarrassing myself.

What happened next was my first lesson in the new era of international television. When I got back to the office to lick my competitive wounds and try to figure out what to do for the morning news programs, I discovered I did not have to worry. People with far greater stature than myself were now dealing with the problem—in part, because I was such a newcomer and, in part, because it is the way important news gets covered these days. An army was on the way. The heavens opened, and equipment and people rained down from the skies. Our sleepy little bureau, which in normal times consisted of myself, a long-suffering Italian bureau manager, and a constantly fretting Italian film cameraman, was suddenly awash with the latest video gear, edit packs, and high-priced producer and correspondent talent.

During the next 30 days, as the cardinals came and went; for the 30 days thereafter, as Pope John Paul I came and went; and for the 30 days after that, as the cardinals came and went once again for another papal transition; I learned a lot about how much television news was changing. First, there were the new video systems. No more waiting for the film to come out of the soup or for restrictions on how much to shoot. (In the film days, people actually used to worry about shooting ratios and about how much film was being wasted. With video, no one seemed to care). Then I learned about money and competition. The right story meant you could spend anything as long as you beat the guy from the other network. The Vatican and I together learned about the clout of network TV. It had been 16 years since the previous papal transition; live coverage from across the Atlantic was not technically possible when Paul VI was chosen and enthroned. But in 1978, it was not only possible to link earth stations to satellites around the globe, but the American network news divisions were putting stories on the satellites practically every day. After some pushing from the networks, church officials came to realize that if they would only permit a few heretics like myself free-run of the Vatican, they could get hours and hours of free coverage, mostly favorable, that would help them spread the message, not only in the United States but worldwide.

Our coverage that late summer and fall also awakened me to something else—with developing satellite technology and the increasing sophistication of broadcasters internationally, the networks were committing tremendous resources to travel anywhere in the world for stories, even if those stories were of limited relevance to American viewers. This was a fairly new development because while Vietnam had launched television news overseas in a major way, it had been a single story that was so important to Americans that any expenditure could be justified. With improved satellite connections and with costs of travel and coverage coming down, the news divisions were beginning to dispatch their foreign correspondents to stories far distant from their home turf. This change did not really become clear to me until several years into the 1980s, when I had lunch one day with one of my predecessors in Rome, Irving R. Levine. I was bemoaning all the nonstop globe-trotting I had been doing in the previous months and boring him with the details of how it was wreaking havoc with my personal life. Typically, Irving's response was a revelation. "You are lucky," he said. "In my nine years in Rome, I only left the country to cover stories nine times." By the time I got to Rome, that was unthinkable. There were times in the mid-1980s when I was leaving home base to cover three different stories in three different countries in a single week.

With the travel came a new set of problems. Irving knew Rome thoroughly, the Italians intimately. I found myself on the road to so many different destinations, I often felt that I was not very in touch with what was going on. Every so often, though, in places like Iran, Beirut, Israel, the Philippines, and others, assignments lasted long enough, or trips came frequently enough that it became possible to get acquainted with what I was supposed to be talking about. Invariably, that was when my reporting was at its best.

Even so, because of language differences, foreign correspondents are only as good as their local contacts. As the travel has become more exotic, and the network reach longer, the news divisions have assembled the names and phone numbers of more and more stringers and fixers, often kept on retainers, who can lend a hand to firemen correspondents in almost any corner of the globe where they happen to land. But the reliability of these local types is sometimes questionable. Some, citizens of countries with totalitarian regimes, could not work for Western journalists without having a fairly well-developed link to the local government. For others, the money that sloshes around a network operation can be a powerful motivation. It is not unknown for stringers to exaggerate a local crisis in order to entice the high-rollers from the networks to come into town, or to get them to stay on a little while longer.

There was never a gathering of network high-rollers like the one that was getting underway just a few months after those papal transitions. As 1979 dawned, the networks were at the beginning stages of what would become one of the most expensive foreign operations they had mounted since Vietnam. The Shah of Iran was in exile, his nation was in turmoil, and a religious extremist in Paris named Khomeini was about to fly home after 16 years in exile. The discontent had been churning just beneath the surface in Iran for years, but no one, not the media and certainly not the networks, had any idea the Shah of Iran might be in trouble. Then in the fall of 1978, an earthquake brought it to the surface. It was my Rome colleague, Quint, a veteran of many revolutions, who I believe was the first reporter to spot the signs. He reported that religious leaders in the earthquake-stricken city of Mashhad were outraged that the rescue effort by the Shah's army had lasted only a few days. His generals quickly gave up on retrieving any more living or dead beneath the rubble and simply bulldozed the whole mess. Quint reported that the lack of proper burials contravened Islamic law and angered the local religious leaders. And there was much emotion, too, over the possibility that survivors trapped beneath the collapsed buildings were killed when the rescue efforts became rubble clearance. The outrage soon spiraled out of control, and before long, revolution was in the air. By November, all the networks had correspondents in Iran continuously.

Back then, we members of the Tehran press corps were enjoying that curious life of luxurious terror, first invented by the press hacks based in Saigon during the Vietnam War. Essentially it consisted of scaring the bejesus out of yourself, running around on the streets or front lines during the day, and then repairing to the bars and dining rooms of a luxury hotel at night for a good meal and a comparison of notes with fellow foreign correspondents. This does not happen much any more. But from back then, I have vivid memories of fine dinners of Iranian caviar, prime rib, and bottles of Bordeaux in the top floor restaurant of the Tehran Intercontinental while looking down on a city literally in flames with the fires of the revolution.

Nothing, before or since, terrified me the way Iran did. I have been shot at and under shell fire in nasty situations from Beirut to Somalia, Liberia to Croatia, but I have never been exposed to anything like the random street violence of Iran's revolution. I will not forget the day as the revolution reached its peak, when the Tehran police chief, stuck in a traffic jam like everyone else, was pulled from his Mercedes. Not a shot was fired, but a crowd of demonstrators a block long vented their fury on him. By the time his corpse reached the end of the street, there were no arms, legs, or head left, just the bloody trunk of his body. Several days later as the Shah's armies finally collapsed, I was outside the military-training school where cadets were firing on loyalist tanks. There was machine-gun fire in all directions. I heard bullets whizzing over my head and felt a ricochet hit me in the back, although not hard enough to do any damage. So, hoping to avoid further unpleasantness, I went up to a rooftop to do my on-camera stand-up. I got one successfully recorded and went for another take when the soundman started waving like a madman and pointing down at the street. One of the revolting military cadets had us in the sights of his M-16. I ducked as he fired. There was never a second take. Later, when I got back to the hotel, I learned that in an apartment just a few yards away, Joe Alex Morris, a veteran reporter for the *Los Angeles Times*, had been gunned down as he stood up for a better look at what was going on.

Reporters take just as many risks, and even more these days, but today there is almost never a luxury hotel to go back to. Technology changed it all. Modern portable satellite dishes mean that TV correspondents no longer have to be near a major city with a functioning television station in order to get their stories out. Today, for better or worse, the media mob becomes a part of the story because the satellite up-links are most often set up as close to the action as possible. What that means is that today's foreign correspondents are very often eating and sleeping in the disaster they are covering. After a recent earthquake in India, one of our Paris cameramen who was sent to the scene, told me that the assembled correspondents and technicians were competing with the earthquake victims for what food, water, and shelter there was available. Given the fat cash advances the network types carry, there was not much question who was going to win the competition. A variation of the same thing has happened during the operation to save the Kurds in Turkey, throughout the war in Bosnia, and in other places where scarce resources are often made even scarcer thanks to the arrival of the press gang.

There is now a new, old saying among TV types: wherever the dish (as in satellite dish) goes is where you will be spending the night. As the equipment has gone farther into the field to get closer to the tragedies and mayhem we cover, correspondents have had to get used to sleeping in tents, doing without hot showers, making a bottle of water last the day, and eating meager rations instead of three-star meals. My friends who covered the civil war in Rwanda lived in a fenced compound with the French Army troops who had been dispatched to the rescue. The TV types said they will not soon forget the horror and smell of waking up each morning with scores of dead bodies stacked up just outside the compound fence, 50 feet from their tents. That kind of close proximity to events means that a certain amount of extra passion is inevitably going to creep into the reports from people who are in a very good position to empathize with the plight of the victims they are covering. This may not necessarily be an altogether positive development.

Among other things, it can contribute to the belief among belligerents in a conflict that reporters are active participants in the story. The concept that journalists are independent, neutral observers who do not take sides is generally accepted in Western democracies, but it is a completely foreign notion in most parts of the underdeveloped world. One of the reasons so many journalists died in Bosnia, particularly in the first year of the war, is that they were actively targeted by the participants—usually the Serbs—who believed reporters to be the enemy.

Another upshot of all the jet-setting foreign correspondents started doing is that their networks tend to think of them as generalists, capable of landing anywhere, covering anything, and eventually beaming back something to New York. As the years have gone by, specialties, language capabilities, and prior experience on a story count for less, as assignments are made, more often than not, using the somewhat random AG/GWAT method (Any Guy/Girl With A Tie). The assignment desk does not worry much about the background of the person who is sent, just so long as someone is standing there clutching enough packets of wire copy to fend off any attack of editorial confusion. This has led to another recent phenomenon, centralized basing. Rather than have small bureaus scattered all over the map, which some money managers believe duplicate resources and—arguably—cost more, the networks (as opposed to CNN) today have gathered correspondents together, primarily in their London bureaus. This may save money, but it also means there are fewer dependable eyes and ears on station out there to pass back their own interpretation of events to headquarters. All of the networks still maintain some offices and crews outside of London, but, as of this writing, in Western Europe, only NBC has a correspondent based in Germany, only CBS has a correspondent based in Rome, and only ABC has someone in Paris (me!). After ABC's Tel Aviv correspondent was reassigned to the

United States, I was, for almost a year, the only full-time, on-air correspondent for ABC News based between London and Antarctica. In 1996, I lost the distinction when ABC moved Bill Redeker from Los Angeles to Tel Aviv.

Along with the centralization in London has come the notion that it is just as easy to cover international stories by sending reporters from the United States. Frequently these days, for summit meetings, trips abroad by cabinet officers, major military operations, and other stories, the correspondents sent to the scene are Washington- or New York-based. This is rationalized by some, who note that the travel has become easier and there are fewer correspondents overseas, but they overlook the fact that it leads to editorial weaknesses. A Washington reporter on the White House beat, for better or worse, pretty much reports the thinking of the White House. That is part of his or her job after all. But in better days, the networks would often cover an international story with both Washington and foreign-based correspondents, because it was believed that a second, outside-the-beltway take on things, might be worth covering. It made for more balanced, less Potomac-centric coverage, and it is increasingly rare in these cost-conscious days. Without providing embarrassing specifics, I have seen some true inaccuracies of reporting from Washington-based correspondents who were temporarily assigned overseas and who tended to cover events a little too closely from the perspective of their stateside beats without getting a good look at what was really going on out in the countryside—as opposed to what their Washington sources said was going on out in the countryside. In Somalia, a colleague of mine who covers the Pentagon had the embarrassing duty of retracing his steps after he filed a story saying what a wonderful job the army was doing making friends with the local population of a rural coastal town. The very day he sent his story, a *New York Times* correspondent reporting from the very same town wrote a front-page piece about the potential dangers facing American troops, quoting a local Islamic religious leader who vowed to kill any American soldier he saw. Oops.

Back in Iran, as the decade of the 1980s was about to begin, the network news divisions were again deploying forces in massive numbers. Americans—and the U.S. presidency—were being held hostage by religious radicals. What a story! In their in-your-face style, the Iranians were in front of the embassy-turned-prison every single day, demonstrating and beating themselves. But not all the self-flagellation was taking place on the streets of Tehran. Back home, the editors could not get enough of it. At various stages of the hostage crisis, the networks had up to four correspondents, each covering the story. (By contrast, as the 1990s began, one of those same networks had only four correspondents totally in all of Europe, Africa, and the Middle East).

The hostage crisis all came to a dramatic—if not sudden—conclusion on Inauguration Day 1981. I would love to know what the three networks spent on news coverage on that single day. While a presidential inauguration is an unusually labor intensive event for the networks, generally requiring hundreds of crews, producers, and correspondents, the live hook-up that stretched from California to Tehran to cover the hostages and their families January 20, 1981, was unlike anything ever seen before. I was standing in the rain at the Algiers airport with NBC correspondent Keith Miller ready to capture the first steps of the hostages into freedom. Coming through our earpieces was a mind-numbing jumble and juxtaposition of history. Between camera calls and profanity from the director, amid the calm, seat-of-the-pants planning by the executive producer, I could hear snatches of sound from around the planet—a bit of "Hail to the Chief" being played, a reporter briefing a hostage family on the latest news from Iran. As the day and night went on, Chancellor, Brokaw, Delaney, Pettit, Oliver, Cochran—and Bittermann—came and went, contributing their bits and moving along as two momentous events took place simultaneously. Weeks later, with a generosity of spirit no one seems able to afford any more, Jerry Lamprecht, then the assignment editor for NBC News, sent each correspondent involved in the special coverage a copy of the *New York Times* from the following morning. "Reagan Takes Oath as 40th President; Minutes Later 52 U.S. Hostages in Iran Fly to Freedom," the headline reads, and it still hangs on my office wall. Seldom was there ever such a global broadcast before—and never have I felt more a part of a such a far-reaching and powerful organization—as that day.

The hostage story and the developing confrontation between the Soviet Union and the United States over intermediate range missiles in Europe only whetted appetites in the newsrooms back in New York. The crystal-clear video that came in from abroad—unlike the grainy and scratched film images of the preceding era—seemed in those days new, fresh, and especially exotic. Both morning news broadcasts and evening programs would, without much argument, buy into trips practically anywhere just because the world looked so much closer on video than it did on film.

So off we went, to cover transatlantic balloon flights, royal weddings, and the opening of Egyptian tombs. In one memorable year, I celebrated the White Russian Christmas in Monte Carlo, watched the first man in history peddle an airplane across the English Channel, spent weeks wandering with Gypsies through central Europe, and traveled around Spain learning how to become a bullfighter—all of it in the name of news gathering. I sold the latter two magazine-length stories, each of which cost well over $100,000 to prepare, on the strength of two words. An executive producer asked me by e-mail if I had any ideas for his summer magazine programs. . . . I simply responded with "Gypsies and matadors." He immediately saw the potential and ordered me to proceed.

A decade later, getting such a decision from a news executive in that way would be practically impossible. There has been a fundamental change—in part, but not exclusively, because of tighter network news budgets—in what editors consider foreign news coverage. Rarely these days do the networks have the time or money for a story that simply provides an interesting look at the distant, curious, or seldom seen, even if that often can provide television's most memorable stories. Today, more typically, budgets and airtime are allocated to foreign stories with edge and blood. Editors share a common belief, supported by marketing surveys, that audiences are not interested in foreign news unless it has violence or direct relevance to Americans. But by slavishly following the audience polls, the editors render themselves irrelevant, since audiences dial-up news precisely because they expect someone to find the unexpected for them.

All the while network news from abroad has been getting harder it has also been getting shorter. People who put their stopwatches to the evening newscasts, like Andrew Tyndall, publisher of the *Tyndall Report*, detect a 45 percent drop in the amount of time given to international coverage since the fall of Eastern Europe and the end of the Gulf conflict. In 1990, the three networks devoted 7,700 minutes of the 15,400 minutes of evening news time to international news stories; by 1995, it was down to 4,200. Tyndall believes the decline is due to a combination of decreasing network news budgets and refocused news agendas after the political changes in Eastern Europe. "The networks took advantage of the international changes to cover more domestic news, which costs a lot less," Tyndall said. One small glimmer of hope he provides to dispel a foreign correspondent's gloom is that since 1992, the portion of the network evening newscasts devoted to international coverage has remained fairly stable, making up between 25 and 30 percent of the evening news airtime. Says Tyndall, the big stories still get covered the way they always have been. What has disappeared are stories of medium importance that were nonetheless very interesting.

Tyndall's surveys of the evening news have pointed out another trend, one that is distressing not just for foreign correspondents but correspondents in general. Essentially he has confirmed what many have suspected for some time—when a network shells out 7 or 8 million dollars a year for an anchorman or woman, it will want that reflected in the amount of airtime he or she is allotted. That helps amortize the cost, of course, but more importantly, the greater airtime reflects the management assessment of the greater marquee value a particular talent has.

Peter Jennings, Tom Brokaw, or Dan Rather draw people into the tent, so you pay them a lot of money, use them a lot so you get your money's worth out of them, and use them a lot because they will, in theory anyway, draw more people into the tent.

But there is only a finite amount of time in each newscast, so if you give the anchor people more exposure, someone has to pay for it in lost airtime. Those someones are the correspondents in the field. Tyndall's surveys indicate that in their own news broadcasts, both Jennings and Brokaw are not only the anchormen, they have also emerged among the top ten correspondents in the amount of airtime they get. In other words, they not only are reading the introductions to stories, more and more they are reporting the stories themselves.

Now, quite naturally, correspondents, especially foreign correspondents, are not convinced this is a good idea because often the story the anchorman picks to do himself is one from overseas. And while reporting a foreign story may make the anchorperson appear worldly and wise, it is quite often the very story that is the most complicated to tell. When the president of France died, I was told that the obituary would be done from New York. The fact that I had covered François Mitterrand from his first day in the Elysees Palace until his last day simply was not a factor in the decision. "The anchorman," a producer told me firmly, "does all 'head-of-state' obituaries."

Faced with declining network interest in international events and declining airtime overall, network foreign correspondents are not a very happy bunch these days. There is still the occasional possibility to throw on the old trench coat and dash off to stories that hold the promise of great intrigue and adventure, but it does not come up as frequently as it once did. What is more, as the video news agencies—AP-TV, Reuters-TV, and World Television News—have become more competent at covering news in their areas, there is a growing inclination on many marginal stories to "let the agencies cover it." This makes the accountants happy, but it also means foreign reporters are getting out of their offices and into the field less and less.

I suspect that the trend will only continue, as will another cost-cutting trend, the use of non-Americans to provide the news you see from overseas. For years, the networks have employed locally hired technical crews to cover international news, but as the go-go era of network news coverage was winding down in the late 1980s, the networks began recruiting producers and now even some correspondents. Locally hired in Britain, France, Germany, Israel, and elsewhere, they do not require the kind of plush housing and cost-of-living benefit packages that North Americans routinely received in the past.

Foreign correspondents who are in fact foreign bring to the networks both advantages and disadvantages. They know well their languages and homelands, but their coverage frequently suffers from a kind of cultural myopia. One American overseas news producer, who recently was moved back to the United States, used to call it "the Skippy factor." Ask anyone born in North America what Skippy is and he or she can readily provide the answer. But a non-American would have had to make a very thorough study of the United States to know the name of its most famous brand of peanut butter. The producer's point was that whether they know it or not, Americans carry a fair amount of cultural baggage. A person who grows up in a particular country shares with his compatriots some common reference points that, without even being aware of them, come out in the way he observes and interprets what is going on around him.

Perhaps the greatest hope for those of us still overseas covering news for the networks is that the networks themselves have changed, venturing into the cable news business. It is a development that demands a much greater effort on the part of news divisions to cover international stories, but on cable TV budgets. The financial constraints will for some time to come mean only limited travel, lower salaries, and perhaps only part-time work for those reporting from abroad. Even so, for the news consumer and those idealists committed to the belief that Americans should know more about what goes on overseas, the network-run, 24-hour news operations and new media ventures, at the very least, mean a little competition for the CNN view of the world. But all that lies ahead.

As for the good old days? Well, they really were pretty good. Nothing will soon compare to a network correspondent's life during that heady time in the 1980s. Did I tell you about the time we flew with Polish crop dusters who were fighting a locust plague in the Sudan? I did? How about this, did I tell you the one about how we chartered a Leer Jet to a South Pacific island? . . .

Epilogue

After the sessions in Carbondale in April 1996 and due in no small part to the persuasive arguments made by my colleague Walt Rodgers, I traveled to Atlanta to meet with CNN executives to discuss working for a network that is still thoroughly engaged in international news coverage. Four months later, I left ABC and joined the CNN Paris Bureau where I am now very happily employed as a correspondent. Many of the problems I focused on during the SIU correspondents' conference instantly disappeared the moment I made the change.

Walt was absolutely right. CNN is a correspondent-driven network with an enormous amount of freedom, a young and energetic staff, and a lean and enlightened management. I am convinced after working at CNN for a year that it represents the future for anyone truly interested in network television news, especially because during that same year, the downhill decline toward irrelevance of news on the entertainment networks only increased. My old mother ship, ABC, in an attempt to bolster flagging ratings, appears to have all but abandoned international coverage, choosing to instead fill its main evening newscasts with "news you can use," a never-ending litany of health miracles, mayhem, and incremental process stories from inside the Washington beltway. I doubt that I will see in my lifetime a moment again like those heady days in the 1980s when the big three networks were really competing to cover the world.

8

The Shrinking of Foreign News: From Broadcast to Narrowcast

Garrick Utley

Television's foreign correspondents do not travel light. Off camera, their distinguishing feature is the small mountain of equipment traveling with them, which sets baggage handlers to dreaming of large tips and airlines to calculating budget-busting excess-weight charges.

The financial burden of that luggage is only one factor making the network television foreign correspondent an endangered species. New technologies in cable and satellite TV have turned the stable, predictable, almost automatically profitable television marketplace into a competitive cauldron in which journalism must increasingly compete with entertainment programming. This has prompted a redefining, or at least a questioning, of the traditional news agenda in the post–Cold War world. Producers and network executives believe the American mass audience's interest in daily events beyond their nation's borders is declining, so little such news is offered—which exacerbates the high cost/low return (or low visibility) nature of international coverage today. On-screen sightings of foreign correspondents grow rarer in the place where the most people would see them—on the networks. According to the *Tyndall Report*, total foreign coverage on network nightly news programs has declined precipitously, from 3,733 minutes in 1989 to 1,838 minutes in 1996 at ABC, the leader, and from 3,351 minutes to 1,175 minutes at third-place NBC.

Reprinted by permission of Foreign Affairs, March–April 1997. Copyright 1997 by the Council on Foreign Relations, Inc.

The Decline of International News (coverage in minutes)						
Foreign Bureau Reports			**Foreign Policy Coverage**			
	ABC	CBS	NBC		ABC	CBS	NBC
1988	1158	1090	1013	1988	597	713	674
1992	1037	736	749	1992	612	509	585
1996	577	692	327	1996	343	446	320
Overseas News[a]						
	ABC	CBS	NBC			
1988	1410	1310	1221			
1992	1166	788	827	*Source*: Data from the *Tyndall Report*.		
1996	918	824	528	[a]Not reported from foreign bureaus; no foreign-policy component.		

A Partnership with the Camera

The image of the correspondent reporting from some troubled land has become firmly imprinted in viewers' imaginations, particularly since 1963. Televised coverage of the assassination of John F. Kennedy bonded viewers to what was beginning to be called a "medium," which could convey human experience and emotions as they could never rise off the printed page. A Roper poll that year found for the first time that television was the main source of news for more Americans than newspapers. Moreover, in 1963, NBC and CBS expanded their nightly news programs from 15 minutes to 30. Some at the networks wondered whether there was an audience—and, therefore, sponsors—for the longer newscasts. More pressing yet, would there be enough news to fill the half hour? One solution was to build up foreign coverage and the role of foreign correspondents.

From the beginning, a television foreign correspondent performed three functions. First, he—it was a mostly male club—was a journalist reporting the story. He was also the report's producer, deciding what events or visual elements needed to be filmed and what interviews recorded to make the story. In the half-hour format, reports initially ran a minimum of two and a half minutes and often three to five minutes, compared with one and a half minutes or even less today. Reports required a narrative line with the reporter as storyteller, which brought up the correspondent's third role, more image-driven than the first two but equally essential: he was a familiar figure who established the news program's "presence" in the story. Merely by being there, the correspondent gave the network credibility, demonstrating to viewers that his organization spared no effort or expense to be on the scene anywhere in the world where important events were taking place.

Almost immediately, however, it became apparent that the correspondent had a partner with a will of its own: the camera. If television's greatest strength was the transmission of human experience rather than facts, analysis, or concepts, the correspondent ran the risk of becoming little more than a caption writer for the moving pictures. Vietnam brought the issue to a head, as sounds and images of Americans at war resonated in living rooms stateside. Even as they enjoyed the status and visibility television bestowed on them, the correspondents in Vietnam found themselves losing editorial autonomy and the pictures' compelling force taking over. Recognizing the immense power of the new visual language, television journalists eventually reached an accommodation with it.

TV Covers the Earth

Then as now, the question facing the foreign correspondent was whether television news, besides offering drama and emotion, could add, if not to viewers' detailed knowledge of the world, at least to their awareness of it. The answer, I believe, is that it has, although the effect is difficult to quantify. Television had an impact on public opinion, which in turn affected the government's formulation of foreign policy, during and after the Tet offensive in Vietnam in 1968, the seizure of the American embassy in Tehran in 1979, the terrorist attack on the Marine Corps barracks in Beirut in 1982, and the killing of American troops in Somalia in 1994. Amid the background noise of the beating of nativist drums and ideologues' declamations, there are few signs that a majority of Americans seek a return to the "splendid isolation" or the Fortress America of the pretelevision era. Many factors have contributed to that relative openness to the world, but TV has played a central role.

The growth of network television news coincided with a broadening of the foreign news agenda. Until the 1960s, correspondents (print and electronic) were based primarily in the European capitals and Tokyo. Those covering Latin America, Africa, the Middle East, and the rest of Asia were allotted few column inches and little airtime, regardless of what was going on in those regions. In the 1960s, however, that changed rapidly, not only because of the longer network newscasts but also because of the growing prominence of the Third World and the nonaligned nations movement, both seen in the context of the Cold War rivalry. The 1955 Bandung Conference, trouble in Indochina, the Congo

crisis of 1959–62, and armed conflict between India and Pakistan in the
1960s and 1970s meant that correspondents could no longer remain in
familiar capitals working their traditional sources. For all the expertise
and language skills they had acquired, news was occurring far from London, Paris, or Tokyo.

Travel became a key part of the foreign correspondent's job description. The advent of the Boeing 707 halved the time it took journalists
to get to another continent. In the 1970s, the routine use of communications satellites made same-day coverage possible, increasing the incentive
for reporters and camera crews to race off to breaking stories in remote
locations. Newscasts saw a marked shift from overseas feature and background stories to hard news. They gained the immediacy of broadcasting
"today's news today," at the cost of the more explanatory coverage that
had been part of the evening news of earlier years.

For the foreign correspondent, instant satellite communications left
little time for developing expertise in a specific country. Reporters became known as "firemen," flying from one international conflagration
to the next. In March 1978, I was based in London, working for NBC
News. On a Monday morning of a quiet news period, I had no plans to
leave the city. By Saturday, I had covered South Moluccans seizing hostages in the Netherlands, the Israeli incursion to the Litani River in
southern Lebanon, and the kidnapping of Prime Minister Aldo Moro in
Rome, and had returned home—three stories in three countries on two
continents in five days.

Cold War Consumers

The mass public in the United States has never shown much sustained
interest in what is happening abroad. Throughout the nation's history,
the American sense of self-containment has rarely been challenged, and
then only by direct threats to U.S. interests. The Barbary pirates' "terrorism," the War of 1812, and the sinking of the *Maine* were international
punctuation marks of the nineteenth century. In this century, too, Americans' interest in foreign affairs has generally been limited to war and the
threat of war. The longest of these conflicts, the Cold War, coincided
with the growth of television, from the late 1940s to the late 1980s.

For those four decades, the East-West conflict was the global environment in which Americans lived. As long as nuclear weapons were
aimed at American communities, the question of personal security took
on an international dimension. Journalists quickly discovered that they
could sell their editors—because their editors could sell the public—
almost any story pegged to a Soviet or communist threat, from crises in
Berlin to Vietnam to Angola. The dynamics were not unlike those in

the defense industry or in politics, where a new weapons system or an anticommunist crusade could always be justified as part of the Cold War struggle.

Afghanistan is a vivid example. In the 1980s the war there received extensive television news coverage so long as the story was about Soviet expansionism. After the Soviet Union's withdrawal in 1989, news coverage in general and network television coverage in particular plummeted, even though Afghan factions were fighting each other with brutal intensity. Not until last October, when Taliban forces occupied Kabul and cameras recorded the excesses of the victors and their vision of Islamic law—hanging bodies and women ordered to stay at home—was the American news appetite whetted again.

The passing of the Cold War era has left many institutions adrift, searching for a new order or definition, and television news is no exception. Without stories from abroad that could be presented as part of an overall threat to American security, newscasts suffered a severe loss in an increasingly competitive medium that thrives—perhaps depends—on drama and conflict to attract and hold an audience's attention. The external threats (say, ICBMs) have been replaced by what many perceive as the threats at home (a mugger on the street corner, drugs, children born out of wedlock).

Paradoxically, broad viewer interest in world affairs is declining from its modest Cold War heights just as U.S. global influence is reaching new levels as the result of several administrations' efforts to expand trade, businesses' need to expand overseas, and the global dominance of American popular culture, all driven by American leadership in the development and exploitation of new technologies. Today more Americans than ever before are working and traveling abroad, from CEOs to sales reps, students, and tourists. International trade is equal to about one-quarter of GDP.

Americans who see themselves as global players (or are merely curious about foreign affairs) find that more international information is available than ever before, from sources targeting smaller audiences. Satellites transmit daily television programs from Europe, the Middle East, Asia, and Latin America to niche and ethnic markets in the United States. One can choose from among on-line computer services or download volumes of free information and comment from sites on the World Wide Web. Television offers numerous business and financial channels and the all-news channels—CNN, which began broadcasting in 1980; MSNBC; and the fledgling Fox News—many of which operate around the clock. The Public Broadcasting Service's *NewsHour with Jim Lehrer* also maintains a journalistic sensibility attuned to international affairs, although it cannot provide much in the way of on-site coverage. National Public Radio and Public Radio International offer extensive international reporting for a fraction of the production costs required in television.

Journalism's Baggage

More than the other news media, television is caught between the declining interest in international affairs and rising costs and competition. It is the most expensive medium for news, and production costs for international reporting are particularly high. A correspondent for a newspaper, magazine, press agency, or radio station or network is engaged in what is basically one-person journalism. He or she can travel to the scene of a story alone, cover it alone, write it up alone, and transmit it alone via telephone, fax, or e-mail.

Television is of a different organizational magnitude. The basic working unit in international television news consists of a correspondent, a field producer, a cameraperson, and a sound engineer, plus some 600 pounds of camera and personal equipment. If a report is to be prepared for satellite transmission, an editor and an additional 600 pounds of editing equipment come along. (Because American television's technical standards are incompatible with the systems the rest of the world uses, the networks must bring all their own equipment.) The cost of this journalistic caravan, including hotels, per diem expenses, car rentals, and local support staff, begins at around $3,000 a day. Airfare and excess-baggage charges can easily reach $12,000. Then there are "extras" like satellite fees. New digital technology, including smaller and lighter cameras and editing equipment, will eventually reduce costs, but there is no indication that the networks would use the savings to increase international coverage.

Network news divisions are currently spending up to $50 million a year on foreign coverage. While only a fraction of overall network news costs, this is an extremely exposed part of the budget at a time when the cost of television news is already under scrutiny. Advances in cable and satellite distribution systems have caused the broadcast news and information market to fragment, spawning fierce competition. Each of the new services competes for market share among attentive viewers who in the past had only the networks to watch if they wanted to feel informed. At any given moment, each of the new channels may have an audience one-tenth or even one-twentieth that of an evening newscast. But together they have cut the networks' share of the television news market approximately 25 percent from the peak years, at the same time that the networks' overall market share has been eroding.

The decline has pushed network news producers to the apparently logical, if journalistically undesirable, conclusion that foreign news is expendable unless it is of compelling interest to a mass audience. The new litmus test at network news programs is whether viewers (in the producers' opinion) will instinctively "relate" to the story. As in other industries, as choice increases, power shifts from the producer to the consumer.

The drive to reduce overseas expenditures has also led to alliances among broadcasters and the growth of television news agencies. The exchange of news video provides worldwide coverage with greater cost efficiency but sacrifices the depth and perspective that an on-the-scene reporter can provide. It is at this juncture that the new competitive pressures collide with the journalistic ethos of the foreign correspondent as well as the expectations of viewers interested in international affairs.

The network news programs and, indeed, news programs in general ought to consider not only whether their response to market forces can sustain good journalism but whether it is a sound long-term business decision. The programs' producers can claim to be focusing on their customers, or at least the largest portion of them. The editorial downsizing, narrowing of focus, and increasing homogeneity of content, however, give viewers searching for broader exposure to the world even less reason to watch the programs. It is a slippery slope.

These days, a television broadcasting company will maintain a costly worldwide operation only if it has a news service that requires (and can help amortize) its international coverage for its audiences in the United States and abroad. The Cable News Network, with its separate domestic and international news services, falls into this category. The new MSNBC (a joint venture of software power Microsoft and NBC) and the Fox News Channel face the challenge of building major international news operations to match CNN. Among the Big Three networks, only ABC News has kept its overseas operation largely intact.

They Reap What They Show

As a few of the most ambitious television news organizations expand internationally, a new shadow looms over the foreign correspondent. With the 1996 merger of Time-Warner and Turner Broadcasting, the parent of CNN, all the major American news divisions are owned by transnational corporations. The financial benefits are clear: Jack Welch, chairman and chief executive officer of NBC's parent company, General Electric, and Rupert Murdoch, who controls Fox, could provide heavy backing for their start-up news channels. Deep pockets count for a lot in the race to create global television empires. But the drive to penetrate new markets and build media imperia raises serious concerns for international reporting and broadcasting. Authorities in the countries on

the receiving end often see the news beamed in as politically or cultur-
ally undesirable, even subversive. When interests clash, as they inevitably
do, good journalism is likely to be sacrificed. The trend is already
established.

Item: Australian media magnate Rupert Murdoch's purchase of
the Hong Kong–based Star TV satellite system in July 1993 was the
keystone of his strategy for dominating satellite broadcasting from the
Pacific to the Middle East. The main attraction was China's booming
economy and potential consumers. Star TV, however, carried BBC World,
the British international television news service. Chinese authorities did
not want the BBC's coverage, or that of any other autonomous television news service, entering China. Murdoch bowed to pressure from
Beijing and dropped BBC news from Star.

Item: In July 1995, the Walt Disney Co. stunned the media world
by buying Capital Cities/ABC. At the press conference announcing the
deal, a reporter asked Disney CEO Michael Eisner how he viewed the
synergy between the two companies. Eisner's response took on a global
dimension: "There are many places in the world, like China, India, and
other places, that do not want to accept programming that has any political content. But they have no problem with sports, and they have no
problem with Disney kind of programming." Political content, however,
is what much of news coverage is about, at ABC or anywhere else. Politics even enters the sports arena, as NBC discovered, and films, as Disney
has been reminded. Last year Disney came under intense pressure from
China not to release a Martin Scorsese film about the Dalai Lama that
the Chinese government believed would be hostile to its claim to Tibet.
Disney announced that it would not back down and abandon the film,
but Beijing had fired a shot across the company's bow.

Item: At the opening ceremonies of the Olympic Games in Atlanta,
NBC Sports commentator Bob Costas angered the Chinese government
with his remarks as the Chinese team marched into the stadium. Costas
said, according to an NBC transcript, "Every economic power including
the United States wants to tap into that huge potential market, but of
course there are problems with human rights, property rights disputes,
the threat posed to Taiwan." Costas also mentioned suspicions that per-
formance-enhancing drugs could be behind some of the achievements of
Chinese athletes. China's state-run media and its Foreign Ministry attacked Costas's comments. A month later, NBC issued a statement
apologizing "for any resulting hurt feelings." The statement continued,
"The comments were not based on NBC beliefs. Nobody at NBC ever
intends to offend anyone." But the Chinese government did not ease its
pressure on NBC, whose owner, General Electric, and GE's partner in
the MSNBC news channel, Microsoft, both have extensive commercial

interests and ambitions in China. The Foreign Ministry declared, "Any news agency in the world should respect and comply with the most fundamental professional ethics and not produce reports which distort facts. It is hoped that NBC will draw lessons and make sure that there will be no recurrence of things like that."

Commercial and other pressures have long been known to have a chilling effect on the independence of reporters and their employers. Increasingly, it will be the foreign correspondent who feels the chill as she or he reports from countries where markets have become free before the flow of information has. Unlike the traditional publisher or owner with whom reporters and editors could discuss a sensitive issue after climbing a flight of stairs, the new owners, because of the vastness of their organizations, are distant physically and in their priorities. Censorship is not a new experience for foreign correspondents. But what they will face in nations whose leaders seek the profits and products of the global market without sacrificing political control can be as effective and more insidious: self-censorship. As GE tries to sell more jet engines to the Chinese, and Microsoft more software, how confident will NBC or MSNBC reporters feel about interviewing dissidents? If Disney builds a Disney World outside Shanghai or Hong Kong, will ABC News producers and reporters have second thoughts about taping an investigative report on corruption in the ranks of Chinese government and party officials? As NBC and Bob Costas can testify, there are no longer hypothetical dilemmas.

Everyone Is a Reporter

The growing tension between journalistic and commercial priorities may never be fully resolved. But whatever direction events may lead journalists, the role of traditional news organizations is likely to shrink further. The flow of information from fax machines to the Internet and through other technologies already developed or still undreamed of will overwhelm efforts to control it. Today and in the future, anyone sending information from one country to another is a de facto foreign correspondent. The number of correspondents, accredited or not, will rapidly increase. Equipped with camcorders and computers, they will send out and receive more and more foreign dispatches. Even in countries where governments try to control the availability of video on the Internet, ingenuity and ever smaller satellite dishes will enable some, perhaps much, news and information to get through.

Given the global commercial and technological changes facing television news, in a world where almost anyone can be a foreign correspondent, what will be the role of the traditional bearer of that name? When the Internet and on-line services offer full-motion video, network newscasts will feel even less compelled to provide coverage of foreign events to a mass audience. But those interested in what is happening abroad will find a selection of information even broader and deeper than cable news channels now offer. Layering of information— video, sound, text, and graphics—will give the news consumer unprecedented choice, as well as editorial control. And the person providing that information could be a new type of foreign correspondent, or perhaps the old type with new means of communication.

Rather than dashing around the world to provide an on-screen presence, the correspondent will be judged on the quality and depth of knowledge he or she possesses. Foreign correspondents will have to be versatile and informed journalists who can write commentary for videotape as well as for print, knowledgeable specialists who closely follow a country, region, or topic and can appear on camera or on line to talk about it and respond to questions and comments. They will have to be able to communicate interactively with an audience whose members will be informed, engaged, and more demanding than the passive television viewers of today.

Those Americans who actively seek more knowledge about the rest of the world and how their country or business fits into it will be better served. Since they will likely be opinion makers—and voters— public discussion of foreign affairs could conceivably improve. Unfortunately, the debate would not include the broader public that is not plugged into the wider world.

What is being lost, or at least weakened, has long been forecast: the role of a few television network news organizations as a unifying central nervous system of information for the nation, and the communal benefits associated with that. Some may mourn the loss, especially those who grew up with network news. (More than half the audience for the evening network news programs is 50 or older.) Viewers and social critics may debate whether the gains accompanying the growing diversity and flexibility of news and information delivery outweigh the losses. But quite aside from the fact that nothing can be done to stop the technological advances, the benefits in choice and content are clear.

It is always tempting to ascribe a utopian future to societies that are being profoundly altered by new technologies. Still, for the fraternity of foreign correspondents, the forces of change could offer a road back to their traditional craft. The foreign correspondent of the future may wear the obligatory trench coat or safari jacket of yesteryear. But underneath it, she or he will have to possess a depth of expertise to satisfy the increasingly demanding, informed, and technologically equipped consumer of the information age.

9

Communication Technology and the Correspondent

Michael Murrie

> *The years before the Civil War were important for the American press. Technology enabled newspapers to reach for a mass audience with timely telegraph news. Technology also decentralized the power of the widely-clipped Washington, D.C., press and likewise accelerated the development of a new position in the newsroom, the position of reporter. As newspapers became one of the nation's first mass-produced products, reporters were needed to ensure that publishers had enough timely information for the voracious news appetites of newspapers now on the edge of expansion in physical size, and after the Civil War, in numbers of pages.*
>
> —*Donald Lewis Shaw,* Journalism History, *1981*

Change a few facts, and Shaw's words would apply to radio and World War II when on-the-scene correspondents such as Edward R. Murrow became prominent. Substitute television news and the Vietnam War and again see how the technology affected mass audiences by bringing the images of war into homes and elevating correspondents, such as Dan Rather or Ted Koppel. You could even note the development of satellite reports and the prominence of correspondents, such as Peter Arnett or Bernard Shaw, during the Gulf War. Each advance in technology and war coverage accompanied a renewed emphasis on the importance of those who gather news.

Recently, however, technology has lead to diminished importance of the people who gather the news in the field. Except for CNN, the television networks have deployed fewer correspondents and kept more central editorial control. This chapter will examine the impact of technology on the correspondent and present a broad review of television news technology.

Shaw's description of the impact of the telegraph on news still has many parallels today. In the mid 1800s, the telegraph accelerated the transmission of text. More than a century later, the new television news technology accelerates the transmission of moving images from the most remote place on earth to any other place. Local television stations rely less on network news, today's television equivalent of Shaw's Washington, D.C., press. Instead, the local stations program their own versions of national and international news often before the network newscasts, using material from syndicated news sources, including their affiliated networks. The local stations sometimes even send their own satellite trucks and reporters to major national and international stories to report them from a local viewpoint. Networks respond by developing more magazine programs and by changing the evening newscast from a headline service into a program with more in-depth reports providing context and analysis.

CNN political and media analyst Jeff Greenfield (1993) says technology may force networks to do the interpretive reporting they should have been doing:

> Networks were born and flourished because of logistics. Now, technology has diminished that power, so networks may be compelled to turn to the one thing that all the technology in the world cannot produce: good writing, clear thinking, varied and rich portraits of the people in the country and the world. (Greenfield 1993, 72–73)

In the last 20 years, the tools to expand the mastery of the television correspondent have tripled. These tools extend the fundamental processes of acquiring images and information, writing, editing, and communicating with sources and editors. Some put a new emphasis on news gathering from the field. Others challenge correspondents to generate new kinds of content and to communicate across cultures. These trends will become evident with the following chronological review of television news technology.

In the last quarter century, television news has experienced three major developments in the gathering and producing of pictures for news stories. The first, in the mid 1970s, was Electronic News Gathering (ENG), the use of portable videotape rather than motion picture film. With ENG came the ability to use portable electronic cameras and microwave equipment to quickly establish live, remote signals. The second phase was Satellite News Gathering (SNG), the development of portable satellite uplinks for live, remote signals. The third, Digital News Gathering or DNG, allows computers to manipulate news content for new purposes.

ENG: The First Wave of Change

In the early 1970s, one person could easily operate the last popular news film camera, the CP-16. The new ENG gear required a camera that was bulkier and heavier than the CP-16 and a portable videotape recorder that was twice the weight of the camera. Even when equipment makers attached, or docked, recorders directly to cameras to create one field unit, the weight and bulkiness surpassed the CP-16. Not until the introduction of certain consumer camcorders of the late 1980s and early 1990s was the equipment smaller and still able to acquire video approaching professional levels.

ENG's initial appeal was not its weight and flexibility in the field, but its long-range cost savings. No longer did news operations need to buy expensive chemicals, film, and operate processors. For the correspondent, the savings meant no restrictions on the length of interviews because of the cost of film. Crews could shoot as much material as they wanted on the inexpensive videotape. Although quality suffered in the first few years, by the end of the 1970s, the quality of news video and the sophistication of editing far exceeded the old film stories.

Correspondents and editors could electronically weave picture stories that were possible, but difficult to do with film. Simple cuts-only, insert-editing systems could separate video from audio and mix two or more tracks of audio on one videotape. Correspondents could precisely control where the audio—natural sound, voices, or music—could rise, fall, or blend. Later, more complex systems enabled certain video effects.

The 1976 presidential campaign was the first to use ENG. Networks were free from film processors and transmission facilities tied to big city stations. Producers could send portable edit packages to the last stop of the day. Deadlines moved from early afternoon to nearly news time. For a short time, there was more time to think and prepare stories, according to Tom Wolzein, a network producer (Yoakam and Cremer, 1985). Then campaigns started to change. Candidates began to make major statements later in the day realizing that later announcements left less time for critical reactions and analysis. To restore some sense of context and analysis for some stories, NBC's Tom Pettit devised a way to tie the latest news with a previously prepared background report.

ENG escalated the competition to get stories on the air quickly. Video eliminated the 45-minute delay of film processing. Once video reached the station, it could go on the air within minutes. The most profound impact of ENG, however, was the ability to quickly establish a live remote report on-scene. Before ENG, engineers needed days to set up bulky cameras and microwave dishes to relay signals from the scenes of stories. The new technology enabled portable microwave transmitters and dishes to be installed on vans or other vehicles. A news operation could dispatch these ENG vans to the scenes of news stories at a moment's notice. In most cases, they could send a live signal within minutes after their arrival. Even helicopters could carry portable microwave equipment and cameras. If correspondents could not reach the story by ground, the helicopter could fly them to the story. Internationally, ENG freed network crews from dependence on foreign film processors. News crews could plug their edit packs directly into the satellite uplink stations. Live interviews and reports by correspondents were much easier to conduct.

Suddenly, it was quicker and easier to establish the technical requirements for the story than the editorial requirements. Correspondents faced a profound new challenge. For the first time, the parties in the television process—the producers and the technicians—were ready to present a story before the correspondent was ready to tell it. ABC correspondent Ted Koppel (1994) described the difficulty:

> Much, if not most, of the process of good journalism lies in the evaluation, the assessment, the editing of raw material. Putting someone on the air while an event is unfolding is clearly a technological tour de force; but it is an impediment, not an aid, to good journalism. Good reporting is to an event what a good map is to a city or to a coastline. It reduces the original in size and accessibility while remaining faithful to the basic features of the original. To simply train a camera on a complicated event is not journalism, any more than taking someone out on a boat and showing them a stretch of coastline is cartography. (16)

Correspondents required an entirely new set of skills to report live because they had to explain to viewers what the live camera showed and why they were seeing it. They had to appear comfortable presenting their stories live, sometimes ad-lib with little or no script. They had to know the history of a story before it happened, be able to explain it as it happened, and instantly edit as they spoke or conducted live interviews. One San Francisco news director in the early 1980s said, "People can give out wrong information accidentally, or they can do it on purpose. All the reporter can do is try to avoid demagogic material" (Yoakam and Cremer 1985, 14).

SNG: The International Correspondent Caught in the Squeeze

The next wave of television news technology escalated the trend to go live at the international level, as well as at the domestic level. The ENG microwave units required a fixed-receiving station to operate. Usually this was on a television tower or tall building in a television station's coverage area. In remote or foreign areas where there were no fixed-receiving points, live ENG was impossible without constructing microwave links.

In the mid-1980s, developments in satellite communication technology extended the range of ENG. New higher frequency Ku satellite transponders made many new channels available for television news coverage. More importantly, the equipment required less bulky equipment than the old stationary C-band satellite equipment. The new dishes and transponders were small enough to mount on trucks. By 1990, hundreds of news operations, including most large- and medium-market local stations in America, had SNG trucks.

SNG gear, called flyaways, could be packed into a dozen carrying cases for shipment by airplane. Theoretically, a correspondent could report live from any corner of the earth as soon as the crew could be deployed. CNN could prepare a flyaway for the road in 2 hours and deploy a dish in the field in as little as 45 minutes. Suddenly, SNG enabled producers of international television news to go live. Who can forget the live images of celebration as the Berlin Wall toppled or the apprehension as Scud rockets fell in Israel during the Gulf War?

However, live capabilities of SNG, demands for more news programming, and a decreasing supply of international correspondents forced a new pace on the remaining correspondents. ABC correspondent Ted Koppel (1994) contrasted the pace of news gathering before and after SNG:

> You write differently when you know that your piece won't make air for another day or two. You function differently in the field when you know that you and your competitors are at the mercy of just one connecting flight. . . . You have some time to think. You have some time to report. You even have some time, while the film is en route to the United States to correct errors.
>
> These days . . . the technological tail is wagging the editorial dog. The network schedule of news programs, or at least news-related programs, is such that a reporter is constantly on call. (16)

Although SNG provides the technology to report from any spot on the globe, political restrictions are barriers to coverage. Telecommunications in most countries is conducted and regulated by government postal/telephone/telegraph (PTT) agencies. Before 1987, broadcasters had to book television circuits a month or more in advance from the local PTT that often provided studios as well as communications links. In the early days of SNG, the PTTs did not know how to react to flyaways, but most PTTs did claim them as within their jurisdictions. Television news crews often encountered delays, hefty fees, or outright bans on the use of flyaways. After all, regulating them was a way to regulate the content of news about the country and to generate revenue.

Gradually, some of the difficulties with transporting flyaway SNG gear across borders dissolved. Deregulation and cooperation among nations in the European Union helped, but perhaps the greatest contribution was a clear statement of recommendations from a subcommittee of the Inter-Union Satellite Operations Group (ISOG), a subgroup of the North American National Broadcasters Association. The subcommittee's recommendations set up an international system of approval of SNG transponders, registration of SNG units, deployment guidelines, SNG contacts, and pricing. One example of the impact of these recommendations was illustrated on President Bush's trip to Madrid for a Middle East peace conference. Many news organizations wanted to bring flyaways into Spain to cover the event. Telefonica initially planned to charge $100,000. Then the price dropped to $5,000, essentially the rate recommended in the ISOG report (Murrie, 1992).

Another kind of satellite news gathering developed during this time, remote sensing or SNG from space. Originally, remote sensing was for military eyes only, but in 1972, LandSat initiated nonmilitary earth observation, primarily for scientific purposes, such as cartography or monitoring crops or weather. The Chernobyl nuclear accident in 1986 marked the first use of these space cameras for a breaking news story, although their use was marred by poor analysis and interpretation. Now remote-sensing images can show the difference between a bus and an automobile. These images have helped illustrate stories such as deforestation of the Amazon rain forest, violations of missile treaties, and Gulf War bombing damage of Baghdad, Iraq. Today's remote-sensing images are available more often and more quickly than in the late 1980s, especially through the Internet. Computers also make analysis of the images easier and less expensive. Radar satellites and special imaging techniques can even see through cloud cover.

DNG: The Future of News

The third major development in the gathering and production of televi-

sion news images has only just begun. Its impact, especially on the correspondent, is unclear. This development began in the 1990s when some
small businesses created new, inexpensive hardware and software to
manipulate video digitally. NewTek, a company in Lawrence, Kansas,
produced a box that for a few thousand dollars could perform nearly all
the functions of a postproduction suite costing hundreds of thousands
of dollars. It was a switcher, a special-effects generator, and a character
generator that also created graphics and 3-D animation. Avid, a Massa-
chusetts-based company, developed a process that enabled editors to use
computers to edit preliminary—and later finished—versions of produc-
tions in a way that dramatically reduced the cost and time required to
edit using expensive postproduction facilities. The new method, called
random access or nonlinear editing, offered the best of film and video
editing and more. Editors could see representations of their clips as if
they were hanging in a film-editing room and could experiment with an
edit with the click of a mouse. They could duplicate edited video without reducing quality. The most frustrating part of video editing, the wait
for the tape to rewind, was gone.

Nonlinear editing, however, was slow to attract interest among
news editors. Many considered it a return to the old film days when an
editor had to wait for processing before editing. Nonlinear editing required a time-consuming, and sometimes tricky, process of digitizing
video. Digitizing was conducted by simply playing videotape for a disk
recorder to make a digital rendering that could be edited by a computer.
In the mid 1990s, equipment makers addressed the delays of digitizing.
Avid introduced a portable recorder that attached to a camera and recorded directly to a hard disk so no digitizing was necessary. The unit
could edit in the field, play an edited module in a live report, and recycle
recording media without reloading. ENG photographers could avoid
missing a breaking news event while reloading tape. However, the portable direct-to-disk recorder had one serious flaw. The price of just one
disk with a capacity of 20 minutes was nearly 100 times the price of a
videotape. Other equipment manufacturers developed ways to preserve
the benefits of nonlinear editing and the economy of videotape, yet bypass disadvantages of digitizing. They developed digital videotape formats
that could be transferred directly to computers at up to 4 times the real
time speed of normal playback. These formats, too, could be edited in
the field on editors resembling laptop computers.

Digitizing video also holds the promise of improving its distribution over distance. Because digital video is just data, it does not necessarily
need to be sent in real time. If the data bandwidth is broad enough,
video can be sent faster than the time required to play a selection. If a
regular telephone connection is used, video can be transmitted using

store and forward systems at rates slower than real time. Encoder/decoders and high capacity phone lines are required to transmit video from the scene of the story to a studio at a rate up to 4 times as fast as real time. Using special equipment and several regular phone lines, or even cellular or satellite phone channels, a minute of video of modest quality can be transmitted in 4 minutes. Digital video makes large SNG trucks unnecessary because digital SNG dishes are small enough to fit on vehicles, such as vans.

Another digital technology is the video server. It is a large high-capacity digital disk recorder that holds video and makes it available to any point on a high-speed network in a television facility. When the correspondent works in the newsroom or the studio, a server can make video available—even simultaneously—to any editor, producer, or reporter who wants to view or use it to edit the video for a story on a newscast, make editorial decisions, promotions, or additional versions of a story.

Initially, the impact of DNG on news content and the correspondent seems less profound than the development of ENG and SNG. So far the only noticeable improvements are higher quality video and more flexibility in the editing and transmission of video from a story to a station. However, over time DNG may open entirely new vistas for electronic journalism.

Already news organizations are enlisting powerful computers to create beautiful new graphics to help tell stories. Many debuted during the election coverage of 1996. Three-dimensional, high-resolution graphics explain stories in new ways. For example, in 1996 when Commerce Secretary Ron Brown was killed in a plane crash in Bosnia, within three hours, ABC News created a three-dimensional representation of the crash in mountainous terrain.

In the late 1990s, television stations will start to transmit digital video and other digitized data. Soon digital video will be shown on wider home television screens that have much higher resolution. Large screens on walls will display television that has the impact of motion pictures. Then what will the impact of television news be?

Future digital video cameras and lenses could introduce virtual reality news. Viewers could see a panoramic view of the scene of a news story and zoom into a portion that seems interesting, or they could choose to see the story from the point of view of a participant. Imagine coverage of a political convention where the viewer could choose to focus attention on a dispute within a state delegation or see the floor from the viewpoint of the speaker's podium. Imagine coverage of a football game where a viewer could choose to watch from a goalpost or from a camera in a helmet. One network producer wants to combine virtual reality news with remote sensing: "I want to grab planet Earth . . . twist it, manipulate it. . . . I want to be able to find what I'm talking about. . . . to fly through it."

Information Gathering

While ENG, SNG, and DNG developed, some less spectacular technologies improved the fundamental processes that take most of the correspondents' time—acquiring, checking, writing, editing, and communicating information with sources and editors. In the last 10 years, time and space boundaries have nearly disappeared. Consider first those now common technologies of cellular phone and fax. Although available, their use was not widespread in the late 1970s and even the early 1980s. Now there is no waiting for a pay phone. A correspondent can talk with anyone from nearly any location. New satellite telephones allow communication from even the most remote places in the world at prices ranging from a few dollars a minute to fifty cents. An early generation satellite phone delivered the dramatic first descriptions of the attack on Baghdad during the Gulf War. A correspondent with a laptop computer and a cellular data connection or satellite phone can transmit or receive a document from any location. The laptop also allows the correspondent to write in the field, submit scripts to editors and producers, gather information from databases of court records or periodicals, communicate through e-mail, or tap the Internet.

Ethical Questions

Each development in television news technology has challenged the judgment and ethical practices of correspondents and their producers. When ENG first arrived, the higher quality video from the field sometimes shocked viewers with the reality of drops of blood on a crime scene sidewalk. Live reporting from the scene of ongoing disturbances such as riots or hostage situations led some critics to charge that this coverage fueled the disturbances. One case that especially attracted such criticism was the looting and fires in Los Angeles after the Rodney King verdict. The ability to go live led to excess. Many newsroom arguments arose over going live for live's sake, even when there was nothing at the scene to see.

SNG only escalated such controversies and introduced some new ones. Video piracy escalated, especially in cases where loyalties were split because of overlapping affiliations with networks, syndicated services, and consortiums of SNG stations. Stations transmitting extraordinary video to their networks sometimes found it on another network or even on a local competing station.

Remote sensing introduces new privacy questions. By the end of the decade, sky cameras will probably be able show an image of high enough quality to read a license plate. If something is visible from the sky, will it be fair viewing for television news?

Digital video introduces new challenges, too. It is possible with the appropriate software to alter video. Colors can be changed and images inserted or removed. Software that uses what is called subtraction technology can even remove a person's image from a live video signal. Fortunately, television correspondents can look to print journalists for guidance because they have dealt with potential digital manipulation for years. Many have concluded that improving quality or correcting technical defects is acceptable, but changing the content of the image is unacceptable.

Conclusion

As the introduction of the telegraph accelerated the pace of news gathering for newspapers in the 1800s, the development of ENG, SNG, DNG, and other technologies accelerated the pace of news gathering and opened new opportunities for innovative coverage. At the same time, the news technologies magnified the pressure on correspondents to quickly and accurately gather facts, analyze a situation, edit, write, and deliver a credible story with little or no time for reflection or even review. The new technologies also introduced new ethical challenges to treat higher quality graphic images more carefully, to be careful about aggravating unrest by reporting it live, to accurately describe satellite images that require expert interpretation, to accurately present the content of an image even when the power is available to enhance or improve the image.

As DNG matures and as emerging news venues, such as the World Wide Web, develop, correspondents can expect new demands on their time, talent, and versatility. Just as they filed multiple versions of stories for radio and television, or fresh versions, they may also have to file additional versions of stories for the World Wide Web. These Web stories may include new elements, such as interactive links within stories or other special images. The correspondent might need to furnish information for viewers to link directly to a source's Web page, or the correspondent might be asked to answer e-mail from viewers. The Web stories might include new image capabilities, such as panoramas. The correspondent would need to write for panoramic images in an entirely different way than writing to moving linear images. Writing to panoramic images would require the correspondent to write short bits linked to certain features of interest in the image. Yet somehow, the correspondent would still need to tie the parts together into a coherent view of not just the entire panoramic scene, but the entire story.

Whatever the technological breakthroughs and subsequent demands on the correspondents of the future, the timeless skill requirements of the correspondent will endure. The correspondent must still have the background from which to understand new events, the perception to clearly ascertain a situation, and the communication skills to quickly use words and pictures to describe the situation in language understood by all. The challenge will be to do all this more often, in a shorter time, sometimes using different message structures.

References

Greenfield, J. 1993. Technology and news. In *Demystifying media technology*, edited by J. V. Pavlik and E. E. Dennis. Mountain View, Calif.: Mayfield.

Koppel, T. 1994. Going live. *Communicator* (June): 16–18.

Murrie, M. 1992. International SNG report recommends lowering barriers for satellite news gathering. *Television Broadcast* (January): 16, 19.

Yoakam, R. D., and C. F. Cremer. 1985. *ENG: Television news and the new technology*. Carbondale, Ill.: Southern Illinois University Press.

10
Dialogue from the Trenches

Introduction
Ed Turner

R emember, please, as you read this section that these four net work correspondents are smart and experienced journalists. Each comes with a frame of experience that cannot be discounted.

As someone who has worked both network and local news, as well as 17 years at CNN, I want to comment about how network news developed into the state these men describe so well.

First, writing as a die-hard newsie, I think the networks should spend money more freely on their nightly news to do a better job of covering the world. They should tolerate a cut in profits and say to the stockholders, "This is the price we pay for franchise." I can well appreciate, though, the reluctance to continue to spend lavishly for an ever diminishing audience to duplicate what other news organizations are already doing. That does not make business sense.

Historically, in the golden years (1962–1985), NBC and CBS, and beginning in the late 1970s, ABC, under the indomitable Roone Arledge, did live—to be charitable—rather high at times. The richly appointed suite of rooms at the headquarters hotel, the limos, and the food caterers did not always contribute greatly to the quality of the story on the television screen. Certainly there was some great reporting done—and some great expense accounts written.

More importantly, as humankind always chases technology so did we in moving from cross-country cable to phone lines to satellite, from black and white to color, and from film to videotape to digital disc. And the technology, of course, changes everything. Whereas there were once no national newspapers, just two and a half national TV news organizations, and many pretty fair weekly news magazines, we now have three national newspapers, five networks, plus fledgling Paramount and Warner

Brothers, CNN, CNN Headline News, CNNFN, MSNBC, CNBC, C-Span 1 and 2, FOX News, NPR, hundreds of radio talk shows, local television stations doing seven and eight hours of news daily, all-night news from the three entertainment networks, the ubiquitous VCR, and now the home satellite dish that delivers 150 channels into your home. This makes for a very different business climate than just 17 years ago when Ted Turner launched CNN.

So, to survive, the entertainment networks had to cut here and invest there. The news audience will never again be what Walter Cronkite could draw on an average evening. There is just too much competition for every kind of viewer, reader, and consumer. "Time, time, time" is what "location, location, location" once was: precious.

News was and is only a smaller part of the video profit picture. What the entertainment networks do well—and what they were created to do—is entertain. As stated earlier, the competition for the viewer seeking amusement and escape is beyond fierce. The movies, books, CDs, and magazines take face time away from the tube.

Now comes the really big (as one entertainer said years ago) unknown: the Internet. We do know that more and more time is being spent by the younger—and some older—members of our populations playing with and working on the computer. We also know many of these were strong news viewers; loved C-Span; never missed Dan, Tom, and Peter; and were the weekend political warriors with Brinkley and Co. We also are learning how these computer users are picking their own news, building their own newscasts, dismissing the stories of no interest that they once would have to sit through or zap on the more traditional networks. And, every news organization employing more than three people seems to have its own Web page and a link to another and larger Web page, and so on into infinity. We know the numbers are enormous. At my own company, the CNN Internet page has received as many as 50 million hits in one day and averages 3 to 4 million hits daily.

Beyond all this, we now live differently. Once upon a time, children and Mom and Dad gathered at the dinner table when the one formally employed household member, Dad, got home. Often around that table they would watch Walter, Huntley-Brinkley, or Frank Reynolds. Mom did not have a job. The kids did not have cars. The dinner hour was nearly sacred. Today, Dad may have two jobs, Mom is working, and the children are married and thinking about moving back in with Mom and Dad. One thing for certain is that they do not gather in great numbers as before and solemnly watch the national news. They want news when they want it: news on demand. Thus, CNN and our other competitors serve the mobile, news-savvy, short-attentioned viewer, zapper ever present.

It is difficult to be too critical of company executives when they cut the news budget because their prime mission is to entertain. The long-range danger is the national news-consuming community will receive lower quality news, controlled by fewer media conglomerates. For now, that is not truly an issue. We are all out there battling like hell for advertising dollars, news viewers, and the ever elusive scoop. In the long term, newspapers and news magazines are in for very difficult times. Already it is no walk in video park.

Finally, the single most influential of our broadcast brothers and sisters is the local newscast at 6, 10, or 11 P.M. And noon, and 6 A.M. to 9 A.M., and Saturday nights, and anywhere and everywhere you look on your local television channels. Yet, many of these channels have succumbed to the most sophomoric, inane, and hurtful kind of journalism: the body-bag/burning-barn school of story selection. For the most part, these stories are meaningless unless you happen to be the person in the body bag or living in the barn. There is more to our society than those events.

This panel of correspondents has worked at the network level for many years and has experienced many struggles and triumphs associated with their jobs. They are open and honest about the reality of their work—from the excitement of covering a breaking story to the long hours spent away from home and family. This stimulating and provocative discussion provides an insight into the world of the correspondent from people who know it best. I would be flattered to have any of these men working with me. In fact, two of them now do.

Discussion

The following discussion was held during the Paul F. McRoy Symposium Network News Correspondent Conference held on April 26, 1996, at Southern Illinois University at Carbondale. Those participating were John S. Jackson III, provost of SIU at Carbondale; Joe S. Foote, the dean of the College of Mass Communication and Media Arts at SIU at Carbondale; Jim Bittermann and Chris Bury, both ABC correspondents; Roger O'Neil, an NBC correspondent; and Walter C. Rodgers, a CNN correspondent.

BITTERMANN: As a foreign correspondent, I've lived through the best of times, from the 70s to the mid 80s when the networks were rich and had little competition. But by the mid 80s a lot of things had changed. Corporations took over companies that had for many years been run and created by individuals. The Bill Paleys and Sarnoffs disappeared. You had corporate boards to report to. Money became a factor in everything.

Until 1985, I can't ever remember having had a discussion with a producer or an executive producer about the costs involved in covering a story. We just didn't think about it. When the money pressures came, things started changing. How much is it going to cost? How many camera days are we going to spend? Can we deliver a story in just two days rather than three days?

O'NEIL: We now have to think about how much a story is going to cost before we go out and do the story. We never asked that question before. We now think very hard about what the audience wants. When I watched a St. Louis station recently, one of the stations said, "It is your news." Hell, it's not your news, but it is a neat gimmick to try and get you to watch.

We are responsive to the audience now because of this fragmentation. There are so many other places to go and watch, if you watch at all. Network audiences are below 50 percent now. We have to appeal to a mass audience, or they're not going to pay me the kind of money that I have come to enjoy. If they want me to do something that they think is appealing, damn well, I will do it. I enjoy my lifestyle a lot, and I don't intend to give it up yet.

But having said that, we are also sliding down a road to mediocrity. We no longer present news that is fair to both sides. Now, we are giving it an edge. The news is beginning to sound like that proverbial guy on the radio who says, "Sunday at Vandemere Speedway." And if you're from an older school of journalism like I am, that is disheartening. Yet, it is a reality of the days that we live in.

BURY: Four years ago *Rolling Stone* magazine did a piece on the networks. The lead sentence was that the networks are "pooped, confused, and broke." I think probably at least two out of three of those statements still hold.

When I joined ABC in 1982 in the Chicago bureau, we had four full-time correspondents, eight full-time field producers, four two-person camera crews, a lighting director, an assignment desk that worked around the clock, four full-time videotape editors, our own couriers, and their motorcycles.

Today, that Chicago bureau has two correspondents, two full-time producers, a freelance, and a guy who answers the phones, covering everything from Canada to Memphis, west to Denver, and east to West Virginia. Domestic news is not covered the way it once was. The networks don't cover breaking stories the way they once did unless they're very big. Sure we'll send camera crews to an Oklahoma City, but it used to be routine to cover floods, tornadoes, and small mass murders. We don't staff that kind of thing anymore because CNN is there and because the local stations are there.

So, if we are going to get on the air now, it is going to be with a different kind of piece, like a trend piece or an analytical piece. But that bread-and-butter network story that was so commonplace for us in the early 80s is gone.

RODGERS: There is very little job security in this business. You're only as good as your last story. Jim and I had those wonderful days together when we would rent a sea plane and fly up the fjords of Norway just to go to lunch at company expense. We were naive to think that those days would last. The bubble always bursts. If you read American economic history, it is always cyclical. If you want to survive in this business, you better learn to adapt. And the only thing you have to bet on and rely on is yourself because everybody else is betting against you.

O'NEIL: And yet, having said all of that, it is still the greatest damn job.

RODGERS: It's the greatest job in the world.

BITTERMANN: He's absolutely right.

BURY: And glamorous, too.

BITTERMANN: There are still times when you can put on the old trench coat, dash off, and make it into a pretty glamorous situation. But certainly they don't come with the frequency they once did.

BURY: Before we write the obituary for network news, we should point out that the networks still reach 25 million homes every night. We are still the most efficient way for an advertiser to get a message across relatively efficiently. And we are still very important agenda setters. When Bill Clinton wants to be cool or Ross Perot wants to be glib, they can get on *Larry King Live*. But when they have got some serious mettle to prove, they go to *60 Minutes*, or they go to *Nightline*. We still have the role, along with the *New York Times*, the *Washington Post*, and the *L.A. Times* of being agenda setters. That is not going to go away any time soon.

There is an appetite. *Nightline* has a very core, loyal audience of between 4 and 5 million a night who will tune in to whatever we put on the air. If there is a big story, like Oklahoma City, our audience will double. The magazine programs are also doing well. We do have a role, but figuring out what it is going to be 10 years from now is pretty tough to do.

The Ebb and Flow of Coverage

FOOTE: Because of the demand for big audiences, there has been the gravitation toward the big story, whether it's the O. J. Simpson trial or the Oklahoma City bombing. There's a tendency to latch on to whatever is the ultimate story and hang on for as long as you possibly can.

BITTERMANN: The curious thing for me coming back to the United States only once or twice a year is noticing that the big-story compulsion is becoming more and more pronounced each time. The newspapers, the magazines, the networks are all on the same story. They cover it in a depth that it frequently does not deserve. A seven-year-old pilot crashes, and the mourning period is weeks long. The editors and managers feel that there is a bounce that one gets by being part of a big story. And you don't want to be the one that doesn't report it.

I am at a loss to figure out how you convince managers and editors that they should go down some other path or say, "I found another equally good story out there that's better than the one everyone else is carrying."

FOOTE: But if you're a correspondent and you're not in the path of a big story, you're basically out of business. In the end, the prestige is conferred on those who get on the air, and if you're not on the air very much, you are not very valuable to the organization.

O'NEIL: It's more than prestige; it is job security. There is a pecking order with the networks; some shows are more important than other shows. If you appear on those other shows, your longevity is probably limited unless you have got someone in the front office who particularly likes you.

At NBC, the premiere show is *NBC Nightly News with Tom Brokaw*. I know a number of correspondents who have tried to make careers out of working for *The Today Show*, but their careers usually end with the next contract cycle because the executives simply don't watch all of *The Today Show*. They do watch every second of *Nightly News*. Your face, your mug, and your voice have to be on that program to have the job security that you think you deserve once you have reached the level of being a network correspondent.

FOOTE: When the new Congress starring Newt Gingrich and "The Contract for America" started soaking up the network airtime, what did a correspondent in Paris, France, do?

BITTERMANN: We watched the tide go out. Overseas bureaus have been hit dramatically in the last few years. The lack of crisis in international stories is one of the reasons we've downsized. In Paris, at one point in the late 80s, there were nine network correspondents for the three networks based in Paris. There is now just one—me.

The networks took advantage of that situation to look very severely at the kind of people they had employed overseas and then downsized them. We're probably about half the size we were 10 years ago overseas at ABC. At one point during the Iranian hostage crisis, NBC and the other networks had four regular correspondents deployed in Tehran. In contrast, about three or four years ago, NBC only had four correspondents in all of Europe.

Except for London, each of the networks has only one bureau in Europe. We no longer have a bureau in Germany or Italy. NBC has a bureau in Germany but not in Italy or in France. This downsizing has affected what all of us do. Andrew Tyndall, who tracks network news coverage with his *Tyndall Report*, says the networks changed their views of international news when the global political climate changed. You had not only an East/West situation that disappeared when the Soviet bloc fell apart, but you also had an increasingly good domestic story in the United States with the arrival of the Republicans.

You might ask, "Where does all the foreign news come from? So, how does it happen that there is foreign news on the evening news if you've got so few people overseas anymore?" Much of it is coming from wholesale news agencies and from in-country local broadcasters who have a new opportunity to supply the American broadcast networks with the material they need to appear to be covering the world.

Command and Control

BITTERMANN: The command and control is much tighter these days than it used to be. New York has an expectation that you're on the phone all of the time from everywhere. You're constantly in contact, massaging the editorial line all day long as the story develops. When you're not, they want to know why. That's something that's really changed. Even in far-flung areas of the planet, they expect that there is cellular contact somewhere.

FOOTE: How does that control affect the quality of life of the correspondent?

RODGERS: Horrible.

BITTERMANN: Well, it is. It has diminished your ability to observe and reflect on things. You're constantly getting feedback of what the AP reporter reported or the Reuters man has just put on the wire. Have you seen the same thing, and can you match that? Nowadays, there is a much greater effort to duplicate what they are seeing from other news sources.

There was a time when you could go off for three days to find the story, figure it out, and report it in your way. Today, three times a day you are supposed to be talking to New York and finding out what they know. They tell you what they think, and you tell them what you think.

RODGERS: That can be an asset for us because the cell phone can help us lead the wire service. If I am out on a story and phoning in material and live shots, the wire services follow us. It is very flattering. The problem is that because of this immediacy on the cell phone, accuracy is sacrificed.

BITTERMANN: The great danger is that you get misled by someone or something.

O'NEIL: We always watch CBS and ABC to see what they've done. If we have beaten them in our own mind, then we have this internal, natural high. Yet, at what expense to the viewer whom we are trying to inform?

  I have a concern that I am going to have to face soon with MS-NBC. As soon as that satellite truck gets there, they're going to expect me in front of that damn camera, and I haven't completed the job of gathering yet. So, how can I report to people what is going on when I myself don't know yet?

FOOTE: How frequently are you doing stories that you want to do compared to what executive producers in New York or Atlanta want you to do?

RODGERS: I have got a 24-hour news window. I can push virtually any story I want through it. And I do. Eighty percent of the stories are my choice.

BITTERMANN: I would say 50 percent, and I think it is always a hard sell. On the networks, you are competing against some pretty tough characters who are out there to grab away as much airtime as they can. You have to prove why the story is going to be interesting. And it's not always possible to justify things. You try, but sometimes you just don't win the argument.

O'NEIL: Ninety-five percent of what I do is what I want to do. I live in the Great American West where pictures are in my backyard. The New Yorkers think it is a feat to go out and get a bald eagle flying down a river or to see a moose walking down a highway. So, as long as I can give them those kinds of pictures, there is an appetite.

BURY: I would say for me it is probably more like 40 percent at best. We only do one topic a night usually, and it is really reached by a group consensus. Then Ted Koppel does what he wants to do. So I am in a unique situation. But it is really a show driven by what the big story is that day.

Getting on the Air

FOOTE: What is the selling process you go through to get on the air?

BITTERMANN: Well, get on the phone and write a memo. You make a firm argument for why you think this story is important. And you have to convince people that it not only will be important but visually interesting and within the budget. There are many parameters involved.

I had an interesting story recently that I am still trying to get on the air. It was about a club that had been formed overseas among men who followed wives overseas and were trying to cope. These men found themselves in the same situation faced by many women for years. Basically, they were clubbing together to find out how to survive in a strange land and where to buy diapers cheaply because most of them were taking care of the kids while their wives were off working. Most of the men were Americans.

I wrote a memo to sell the story. A couple of weeks later when it actually came time to do it, New York said, "No, we better hold back because we have enough of those kinds of stories." So I held back for a while. Then, I resold it, and it was accepted. I was about to go off and do it. Then they said, "No, maybe you better hold back a little bit." So, it may yet get done, but it is a process, especially on a story that is totally discretionary. It's a question of convincing people who produce the programs that they should put you on the air.

O'NEIL: It runs the gamut from as easy as a phone call to New York saying, "There's been a snowslide at a village at a ski resort"—an instant two-minute story—to my having to scream at my producer saying, "Who the hell in America wants to see how French drink wine when they can see how Americans mine coal."

BITTERMANN: This is short sheeting your fellow correspondent.

O'NEIL: It is called survival. Sometimes there are perfectly legitimate stories that you simply cannot get on the air no matter how important they are. We had an executive producer for *Nightly News* who simply had a thing about children who were handicapped. And I could not get a story on the air about those children. It was just impossible.

FOOTE: Roger, when you say that you can sell a snowslide in an instant, doesn't that say a lot about network news priorities gravitating toward the dramatic and catastrophic?

O'NEIL: It is the nature of the beast. We will never see the day when we don't do the dramatic story. It is what gets people to watch. I would defy you to argue the point that a snowslide into a ski village filled with people isn't more interesting than doing an interview with a modern-day Henry David Thoreau. Television is a picture medium. It's our job to bring those pictures in the most dramatic and interesting way to the viewers.

BURY: There is an old saying that had the networks been around in Jesus' time, we would have covered the crucifixion and ignored the dawn of Christianity. There is a certain amount of truth to that.

RODGERS: But there is no figuring what they like. No story is innocuous. I did a story just before Christmas that I thought was the most innocuous story in the world. We went down to Bethlehem where I did this story on the dwindling Christian population among Christian Arabs in Bethlehem and how Bethlehem, one of the holiest of Christian shrines, was being taken over by Islamic fundamentalists. I was walking the streets and talking to businessmen who tend to be predominantly Christian Arabs, Christian Palestinians. I worked it real hard before we ever took the camera out. In 30 years in the business, I have never gotten so much hate mail or response to a story. There is just no figuring. The little dinky thing that we put out and think nobody cares about, people care about. And the big ones, the ones you think you have done this wonderful job on, nobody remembers.

BURY: There was a story by another correspondent on *Nightline* that the executives absolutely hated. It was about pensions, personal savings, and 401-Ks. Every single day that the story came up, our anchorman and executive producer found a reason to do another show. Finally after weeks and even months, on a terribly slow news day they had to throw this pension story on. They were groaning and kvetching about it all day, and it was the single most requested transcript in the history of *Nightline*.

BITTERMANN: The executive producers will sometimes have a particular thing that they like or don't like, and you will find yourself covering those kinds of stories because of it. It's not exactly a democratic process. The executive producer is there to make choices and guesses about what he thinks most Americans would be interested in watching or seeing. Very often they don't get it correct. They try their best nowadays using marketing surveys tɔ determine what people want to see, and even with the surveys, I don't think they get a very accurate idea.

FOOTE: In the early 80s, there was a story about a famine in Africa that was turned down repeatedly by the networks. NBC finally purchased a feed from the BBC showing the starving children in northern Ethiopia. It ignited the passions of a nation, but it was a story in which hardly anyone at the network was interested.

BITTERMANN: Any story anywhere in the world can be made interesting if it is done properly and the right angle is found. I am convinced that Americans are interested in absolutely everything. It is often a question of getting past this middle man to get it out to the American public in a fashion that's interesting. What made the Ethiopian situation particularly dramatic was that the BBC reporter on the scene did such a wonderful job of portraying the situation that it convinced the people in New York in a minute. When they put it on the air, the response was unbelievable. Then, we all went off to Africa.

Power Relationship

FOOTE: Because correspondents are dispersed all around the world, is there any real opportunity to speak with one collective voice to management?

BURY: Well, there is no hope for two reasons. The first is the correspondents don't get together. The second reason is most of us belong to a union that provides jobs for out-of-work actors in Los Angeles. The union has no power, and our individual contracts sign away all of our rights to a normal life. So, there is little chance for any collective power.

Individually we have whatever powers of persuasion and political connections we can hang onto.

BITTERMANN: There was a time when you did have some input, but the correspondents' power within the network is diminishing. We used to have an ABC correspondents' meeting overseas, but the last one was in 1989. I think they discontinued them partly because of money, but also sometimes they degenerated into bread-throwing contests and things like that. But, at least they were a vehicle for getting a point across to management.

Nowadays, there is more and more detachment from the New York side vis-à-vis the correspondents. They're less interested in hearing what the correspondents have to say primarily because we tend to say things they don't want to hear.

O'NEIL: I have been with NBC now for 18 years, but in all of those years, there has never been a meeting of correspondents. They clearly do not want to hear us bitch because when we get together, we do a lot of that. The power we have is to propose stories. But once the story is bought or rejected, you lose all power.

They're only interested in you for your ideas, then the final product.

They're running the ship, and nobody is forcing me to take the paycheck every two weeks.

BITTERMANN: The real strength and the real power that you have in this business is ideas. If you've got good ideas, they still can open doors in all directions.

O'NEIL: The power is somewhat determined by how long you have been around, how much they respect your work, and what they think of you.

I have the extra advantage in that I have a big-boy voice. I can intimidate people with my voice over the phone. But a lot of people don't have that ability.

Running the Producer Gauntlet

RODGERS: ABC, CBS, and NBC are producer-driven networks. I work for the only correspondent-driven network where producers and anchors are secondary and tertiary people. In the almost 30 months I have been with CNN, I have had the news division call me and solicit my opinion, accept it, and say "That's a good idea." Unless it is terribly expensive, they buy it. We are just a very different animal from the other three. But it really is a delight to work in that atmosphere. It is very good for morale.

Sometimes on our network, correspondents have too much control. Our script approval process is very porous. But in my bureau, I insist that no script get on the air until I show my script to my colleague. He shows his script to me. We share it with at least one of the other two producers in the building. When we have a script we all agree is editorially sound, then we send it to Atlanta, and nobody ever changes a word. But, we're in a very unique situation. We can't make editorial mistakes in Jerusalem because the Arabs or Israelis will eat us alive.

O'NEIL: It probably works better this other way because you have people who are on the ground where the story is taking place looking at the script as opposed to somebody in New York or Atlanta, so far removed from the story that their input into the story is more superficial.

BITTERMANN: Just to give you an idea of how it works at ABC, I had a script recently where it went through five different rewrites between 1 P.M. New York time and 5:45 P.M. New York time.

The first person who saw it was a foreign producer who had not been out to lunch. He looked at it and said, "I think you should do this and maybe add this." He actually commissioned some shooting to add an American angle to the piece that we were doing.

Then another person would come back from lunch, and he or she would look at the script, and I would have to rewrite it again. And a third person; we went through five rewrites. The fifth person, of course, was the anchorman who came in and took out the American angle that we had put in at the beginning of the day. So at the end of the day, I had a script that bore no resemblance at all to what I had started out with and what I would have filed.

BURY: And so any kind of individual style that Jim is really famous for is gone. In that great Cuisinart in New York, a lot of creativity gets taken out because we have a committee editing system. And individual style is the first thing to go.

RODGERS: Particularly when you do something like an "American Agenda." You cannot believe the rewrites that an "American Agenda" goes through. I think Jim is Shakespeare if he only got five rewrites on that one piece. I have seen scripts tinkered with for two weeks where one individual in your company would make a change and then change it back to the way it was.

BURY: It is an abominable process.

BITTERMANN: The magazine shows are not isolated from this. Some of those scripts will go through 16 or 20 rewrites. And when I talk about rewrites, I am talking about a full edit.

O'NEIL: You run the risk of really making some mistakes because the original writer of the story gets so frustrated with this constant rewriting that eventually that person says, "Whatever you want. Just give me a final version. I'll track it. We will edit it. I don't care anymore because I have lost touch with the story. Do whatever you want."

FOOTE: If you are going live, do you have more control?

O'NEIL: It's the one advantage of going live. They can try to tell you in your ear what to say before you say it, but they haven't tried that with me yet.

BURY: In terms of style, news executives really never touch us at *Nightline*, which is a light-year difference we have.

O'NEIL: One of the difficulties I have is that the producers in New York going over the scripts are looking at words. I am looking at words and pictures. Television is supposed to be a medium of pictures. If you can't tell a story with pictures, you shouldn't tell the story. Yet, in the script approval process, they will tell you to make changes that you don't have pictures for. The orderly process of telling the story with pictures is lost. The value of television is the pictures we put on the air.

FOOTE: What can the networks do to take advantage of your experience?

O'NEIL: Our opinions, our experience, our knowledge have less weight than they used to. There is more second guessing of what we do by those who have never been in the field or have been so limited in their field experience that it is almost laughable that they're telling us how to craft stories.

I value their opinions in New York as a first reader or viewer of my story. But to tell me how to craft the story is wrong when I am there getting dirty, doing the long hours, and reading as much as I read about a particular story before I write it. They just don't seem to respect the knowledge that we have and take advantage of that knowledge.

BITTERMANN: This centralized control is growing. Part of it is because of technology. Part of it may be because they want to make sure it gets on the air and looks like something, and the pictures are in place. And they want to make sure to avoid inaccuracy. But the correspondent in the field is less and less in control of what he or she is doing, and that is frustrating.

O'NEIL: The bosses in New York truly live in a sheltered *New York Times* world. And they do underestimate what people want. I will give you an example at NBC. We put Norman Schwarzkopf under contract, and now once every other week, he does what we call an "American Hero" segment. It is about an individual or group that is making a difference in their community. The response from viewers has been overwhelming. Maybe it is because viewers have been screaming at us for all of these years, "We want good-news stories." To see a network do a good-news story with a true American hero who happens to have "General" in front of his name, makes it successful. But my guess is that that kind of story has a more important place in the newscast than we have ever given it before. Hopefully, if people continue to write and respond to those kinds of stories, you will see more of them because we do respond. We have to respond now to what the viewers say they want and don't want.

The Big Foot Syndrome

FOOTE: Not only have you had executive producers determining when you get on the air, but the anchors are encroaching on your territory. These are very big feet, indeed, coming into the news world.

BITTERMANN: Not much you can do about them. We have all been big-footed before. Big-footing is when a correspondent more senior than yourself comes in and decides that they want to do the story rather than you. Occasionally, I've actually big-footed somebody, but I try to do it as gently as possible.

The anchors now at both NBC and ABC are the top 10 reporters as well as the anchors. That means they are not only reading the intros to the stories, they are doing enough stories to rank them among the top-10 appearing reporters on their network in the evening newscast. That's a change. But the networks pay the anchors multimillion dollars every year to bring news to viewers, and they want to maximize return on that investment by getting the most out of the anchors. Because anchors bring people into the tent, they get on the air frequently.

RODGERS: I have the luxury of working for the only correspondent-driven network. We've all cursed the bane of executive producers here. Executive producers make or break correspondents, but at CNN, the anchors are small fish, especially in terms of the pay. CNN pays its anchors dirt compared to what it pays its top correspondents. My colleagues have to be very careful because to offend Tom Brokaw,

Peter Jennings, or Dan Rather would be suicidal. It is a very tough world out there having to deal with these gigantic egos.

FOOTE: Speaking of Peter Jennings, ABC had a longtime correspondent in Paris, who covered François Mitterrand from the day he took office until the day he died. This correspondent may have been the most knowledgeable source anywhere in the network news on that particular story, but you did not see him doing the Mitterrand obituary. You saw Peter Jennings do the story.

BITTERMANN: I called back to ABC, and I said, "Well, so what are we doing tonight on the Mitterrand obit?" I was told very succinctly that the anchorman does the world head-of-state obits, something that I had not known before. But, it is just the way the business is.

RODGERS: Excuse me, but isn't the public shortchanged? Jim Bittermann should have done that story.

BITTERMANN: I can feel that way. But we are all prey to these marketing forces today that we weren't 10 years ago. These are businesses. And once the news division started making money, it changed a lot.

O'NEIL: The truth is that when we bring a group of people into a room and hook up electrodes for a q-test, Jennings gets more sweat out of people than Bittermann. So, that justifies, to some degree, Jennings's salary and his ability to big-foot Jim on a story. But the flip side of all of that is that on a Friday night when you're big-footed by someone like Peter Jennings, Tom Brokaw, or Dan Rather, and there's a follow-up story to do on the Saturday morning that requires you to stay up all night, suddenly the big-foot correspondent has gone home, and you become awfully important because they want you to do the Saturday morning story that you weren't qualified to do Friday night.

FOOTE: What is the advantage of a correspondent on a beat reporting rather than an anchor?

O'NEIL: The advantage is to have someone knowledgeable with the area who doesn't have to take a lot of time to figure out, in the case of the Freemen, for example, how that town of Jordan, Montana, was reacting to those people for the months before the FBI finally moved in. To have someone knowledgeable about the state, to understand that leave-it-alone attitude that comes with local knowledge—that's the advantage of having a correspondent who is familiar with the territory doing the stories. He can provide insight to viewers from southern Illinois who may have never heard about Jordan, Montana, or the way the people think there.

BITTERMANN: When the anchors cover stories, they flip that around. On an overseas story, the anchors may have a better feel for what Americans want, while the foreign correspondent may know more about the local situation than anybody back in New York does. So what I am hearing down from the phone from New York, I have to assume is a better reading of what Americans are thinking about and interested in than what I can provide from my myopic view from Paris.

FOOTE: Are there correspondents by the force of their reporting who can command viewers, or is that purely an anchor phenomenon?

BITTERMANN: The viewers do not tune in for us. The belief is that the anchor makes the difference. There is clear pressure on Peter Jennings to be on the air as much as possible. They want him to do the special broadcasts, the live shots. They want him to be on the scene as much as possible. If the marketing doesn't show it, at least the prevailing wisdom is that the anchorman makes the newscast.

Overseas, there is a tendency now more than ever to report foreign stories from Washington. While the Washington perspective on foreign stories is important, very clearly there is another perspective that should be called into play in many instances.

For many of the G-7 Summits, there was always an effort to bring in the local angle, the European or Asian side of things. But, the tendency now is to exclude the reporters and cover the whole thing with the White House or State Department reporters, who are very capable but are coming from the American government viewpoint.

FOOTE: Some of my research has shown that a growing number of international stories of the networks are covered from the White House, Pentagon, or State Department perspective.

BURY: Part of it is getting their top-name correspondents on the air a lot because there is a sense from the New York producers that that is what they want.

RODGERS: Does that come at the expense of news?

BURY: It probably does. But if they have a choice between Brit Hume packaging something from the White House and a correspondent somewhere else, they will often prefer Brit Hume's take on it.

Technological Imperatives

FOOTE: How has technology changed the role of the correspondent?

BURY: The satellite changed everything. The live shot and the live satellite lengthened the workday. There were more demands for pieces the same day. When I first got to the network, how a piece was written was the most important thing. The premium in the last few years has been on the live reporter, the one who can be glib and quick on the scene.

BITTERMANN: Because of the time differences, we don't do a whole lot of live stuff from overseas, so we still have the time to craft pieces.

Satellite and ENG (Electronic News Gathering) technology have increased the appetite for overseas news in some ways and also increased capability. The satellite dishes now go further and further into the field. There was a time when we always were bound to a capital city because in most countries that was the only place you could feed from. Now we can get closer and closer to the story; sometimes living on top of the story, as in Kurdistan and Rwanda. Where earthquakes, coups, and crises happen, the satellite dish is there, for better or for worse.

When you're sleeping with the story, that brings about a certain amount of intensity that might not be there if you had the detachment of an hour's worth of thought while you traveled back to a capital or some place. There is an expectation now that you always get the truth back somehow from anywhere.

O'NEIL: It truly has revolutionized the way we do business. It has changed every aspect of what we do. Indeed, the SNG (Satellite News Gathering) truck, the Marti units, the cell phones, the satellite phones have made news immediate.

In another way, the technology has hurt. There is not as much emphasis on the written word. NBC used to have an English expert on staff for *Nightly News*. His sole job was to go over scripts and find the errors. He was a busy fellow, at least he was with my scripts. He is gone now. No one looks at that anymore.

Technology has tied us down. I am now so tied to the computer that when the computer fails, I don't know what to do. I've forgotten how to write longhand. If I am forced to write a script on a legal pad, it is like, "Holy criminy, can I do this? I can't get this done in time." So, it is the good, the bad, and the ugly. My suspicion is that we haven't seen anything yet. The revolution is still coming.

RODGERS: The greatest technological change I have seen in the last 20 years in the business has been the ability to go anywhere fast and throw up a satellite dish. In Moscow during the first week I actually joined CNN, there was a revolution in the streets. We were broadcasting outside Yeltsin's door inside the Kremlin within 45 minutes after they let us in Spasskaya Gate. I had never seen the immediacy of that before. That was mind-boggling.

It is so fast. You're out there with the damn cell phone, and you're on that phone for half an hour or an hour until the dish gets there.

BURY: I happened to be the first reporter on the scene at LaGuardia when the USAir plane crashed in 1992. I was tethered to the live shot. They wanted me live every 20 minutes. I had some young intern from the desk gather information because I couldn't leave the post. I couldn't do my job of reporting because I had to be live all of the time.

BITTERMANN: I wondered what was going on, for instance, when CNN was covering the White House revolution in Moscow. Most of the correspondents were on camera all of the time. There were very few who were out gathering news.

BURY: But look at the Gulf War. NBC had the "scud stud," Arthur Kent, and we had Bill Redeker, who did all of the live stuff, and the rest of us did tape stuff. But, he was the live guy; he was on all of the time. There was no way for him to go out.

O'NEIL: The challenge then is how do you continue to report while appearing in front of that camera all of the time? There has to be an answer to that question, or otherwise we're no longer reporters.

FOOTE: There are vast areas of the world that are under-covered by the American networks. CNN has bureaus in Kenya and India, for example, but ABC, CBS, and NBC have nothing from Cairo to Johannesburg in Africa, or in South Asia, where more than 1 billion people live. As you cast your net every day for news, what is the effect of having those areas uncovered?

BURY: We have been a Eurocentric country for a long time. And that's why foreign resources have been committed to Europe in a way that they haven't been committed elsewhere. Until executives see the kinship of Americans—who are very isolated people who very often don't have direct interests abroad—they are not going to cover that news.

RODGERS: American provincialism is just a residual of the fact that we have two oceans. It is changing, and it has to change. And, as Jim points out, if a correspondent goes out and turns a good story, it doesn't matter where he is; he can get it on the air. The problem is getting the resources to go out and do it.

JACKSON: There are very few dark places left in the world. The Russians know more about what's going on in the outside world because of satellites, the Internet, and other technologies. Still, there are places, like North Korea, that are almost as closed as ever. Will some enclaves always remain in the dark? Or will light and communication always get in, making people unhappy with their lives and wanting something better and different?

BURY: I'm deeply skeptical that changes in communication will necessarily bring light to the world. They might bring information, but light is something else.

RODGERS: British publisher Robert Maxwell once told me that the Communist leaders of the former Soviet Union were scared to death of the satellite technology because of the political and social change it could bring. I think technology does influence these people.

It's difficult to get into places like Riyadh, Saudi Arabia, where they don't want you. And Africa is a hard place to work. The leaders in Lomé, Togo, for example, won't let you out of the damn hotel with your camera. How can you cover a country where you essentially have a police state?

BITTERMANN: The networks are going to have a big surprise when they get into these 24-hour operations. CNN has mastered the art of going live very quickly from locations. I think especially overseas, we've got a lot to learn about that. I remember seeing a news conference in Paris where within 10 or 15 minutes, a live truck was pulling up for the CNN broadcast. I'm not sure we could have done that.

RODGERS: But, you can't believe how zoolike it is. It looks great when I am standing on the air there, but I have no earpiece and have the producer waving. We do it fast. It may look smooth, but it's sloppier than hell sometimes.

As soon as your correspondent loses control in the field, the product suffers. So many of those BBC World pieces, however well written they are, don't have the feel, the energy, and the flavor that the correspondent communicates when he does it from the field. You want the editor in the field to cut your stuff.

We have our shooters edit; our sound people edit; everybody does something. Virtually we go nowhere without an edit pack. So, we edit the packages in the field. You may say, "Boy, that sure stretches those guys thin," but actually if the producer knows how to be a correspondent, we're that much stronger. The cameraman is a better cameraman if he knows how to cut. A cutter is a better cutter if he shoots his own pictures. We are going to see more and more of this multitasking.

BITTERMANN: Nothing would give me greater pleasure than to be able to cut on my computer, and I think we are coming to the day when that will happen.

American Versus Foreign National Correspondents

FOOTE: What is the difference between a network sending a correspondent like you to a location and buying some footage from a news agency?

BITTERMANN: First, the kind of story that you would likely buy from an agency like Worldwide Television News or somebody else is usually a dramatic one, and almost always a violent one. Stephen Hess of the Brookings Institute points out in his book on international news that more than 50 percent of the foreign news that you see coming into your living rooms is violence related. Viewers must think that there is a horribly violent world out there full of coups, earthquakes, and wars. It just isn't so. So, the kinds of things that make foreign news today tend not to be an accurate depiction of really what is going on on the other side of the pond.

Occasionally, we get a request for the kind of story we would do ourselves as opposed to an agency. We got a request recently to compare the social-support systems of France and the United States. When I started putting things together, my editors in New York were amazed when I said, "Hey, they get five weeks of vacation; they work a 39-hour week. They can retire at 55—40, if you happen to be a ballet dancer." There are all sorts of things that are completely unknown here in the United States that would be highly interesting for Americans, but these stories rarely get reported.

RODGERS: That is a function of a network that has a 22-minute news broadcast. Not counting commercials, we do news for 24 hours every day. I run a bureau, and I decide what stories we put out. Even though we are in the Middle East, no more than a third of our stories involved violence in the last year. I have done at least two environmental stories just because I like to go out and watch birds and shoot pictures of birds, and we put on some lovely stuff. We did an Easter story. We have done Passover stories. We mix it up. But that's a function of our larger news window. Much of what we do is political and social.

You would be surprised how many people like things other than stories that bleed. Look at you, Chris. You do environmental stuff. You're really hot at your network. It isn't because it bleeds; it's because people care more than our bosses give them credit for caring about something other than blood. In Carbondale, the two stories people remember that I did most recently were the Easter Jesus story and the environmental story we did in the Hula Valley. And I think people do care about that. But, what we have to do is ram it down the bosses' heads and convince them that there are other stories out there.

FOOTE: What about the trend towards using local talent as correspondents in certain countries as opposed to sending an American? What are the pros and cons there?

RODGERS: I work with an Israeli correspondent, a South African Jew. He helps me enormously because he provides local perceptions and insights I don't have, but it has to be balanced. He values me as an outside person with an American perspective. He gets much more grief from Jews on his reporting than I get from mine.

When Jerrod talks to his mother in South Africa every weekend, she tells him that my reports are much more balanced than his. He sometimes has to feel he has to bend over backwards to be fair to the

Palestinians because he's Jewish; whereas as an American, I can stand back, be detached, and call them like I see them.

If you can have two correspondents in the bureau and balance the perspective, I don't see anything wrong with it, as long as there is an understanding on the part of the second-country or third-country national of what the American news standards are.

BITTERMANN: There are definite advantages because the cultural knowledge and language knowledge are often very important. But there certainly is a disadvantage. They might not understand the demands of American television and get very frustrated when dealing with New York because they just don't understand what American television is about.

There can be a different set of ethical values and principles involved in the kind of reporting that comes in from overseas. The way the French and British press approach stories is entirely different than the way an American journalist would. I am not so sure that it would be a positive thing if a lot of news coming from overseas were strictly from international correspondents who were really international in the sense that they were born overseas.

I don't think you want a correspondent to be a big part of the story. Yet, the satellite dishes going into the field have made correspondents part of the story. Hiring people who are locally involved also makes the news organization part of the story. The more you can avoid that, the better you are.

FOOTE: Occupationally, is it a threat to the correspondent if the networks hire someone overseas for half the price?

BITTERMANN: There are a lot of Americans you can hire for half the price.

RODGERS: As long as you're good, you make it. If you're not good, you don't make it.

BURY: With these 24-hour news services coming up, there is a real threat of a two-tier wage system, similar to the airline pilots, where they're going to be hiring young people with probably a lot less basic experience. They're going to hire them at probably half of what they pay us or less. That is going to put some downward economic pressure on correspondents.

FOOTE: At CNN, there already seems to be the beginnings of a two-tier system internationally where foreign international correspondents are hired in their own countries for much less.

RODGERS: They can't do that in the major bureaus. It won't work.

You aren't going to hire a local Russian for Moscow, a local Chinese for Beijing, or a Jerusalem correspondent who isn't a reasonably heavy-weight American. You may be able to do it in secondary bureaus, but you aren't going to be able to do it in your major diplomatic posts.

BITTERMANN: The biggest shock, by the way, for the BBC reporters who do end up on our air is script control. When they go through the process of four or five people looking at their scripts, they just don't believe it. Some won't do it.

They have absolutely no script control. The BBC correspondent, whatever he says, whatever his values, ethics, principles are, and how they impact on his report is what goes. No one checks his accuracy or the way he has gathered his news.

We have checks and balances coming out of our ears. There are more checks and balances on us than you can imagine to make sure nobody is cutting any corners, and we have the grammar correct.

Permanent Location Versus Parachuting

FOOTE: How much do you think living in a particular environment 24 hours a day influences your reporting?

RODGERS: I am not necessarily a geographic determinist, but I believe that where you live should give you the perspective of the people with whom you live and, thus, enable you to get inside their heads and report on why they behave the way they do better than if you were parachuted in from London or Paris.

BITTERMANN: The longer I am on the story, the better my reporting gets. The longer I am in an environment, the better I get a feel for it.

Most of my reporting is not done in France. In the countries that I know best, I do a better job. I know Germany pretty well because I go there a lot. I have been to Israel and Russia a fair amount. Those kinds of stories I can get a feel for much more quickly than when I arrive in Tunisia or some place I haven't been in a long time.

I was sent out to Japan for three or four weeks and was at a complete loss. There was absolutely nothing to hang onto there in terms of my previous experiences. I couldn't even read the street signs. I was sent around town with stickum labels on me like a piece of Federal Express baggage because I couldn't address the cab drivers. I was a total loss.

RODGERS: I think living there is what makes my job so absolutely exciting and intellectually challenging. I lived five years in Moscow—1984 to 1989—the end of the Cold War to the emergence of Gorbachev. I've forgotten more about Russia than most university scholars could know or teach. It is because I used the five-year period as a graduate seminar in Russian and Soviet studies.

Now I am beginning the same process in the Middle East. You cannot do half as good a story as a correspondent if you don't live there, work there, and even speak some of the language. You have to know the suffering of Palestinians to report on them. You have to go up the West Bank a couple of times a week. You have to understand the insecurity of Israelis to know and report on it. That's basic.

FOOTE: When networks close half of their foreign bureaus and are stretched so thin that they must travel thousands of miles to get a story, what does that do to the quality of reporting?

BITTERMANN: You just can't do as good a job parachuting into a story as if you are there to begin with, and you see the story coming, and you know the background and the rest of it. The best reporting I have done is when I have had the opportunity to continue the same story for weeks or months. You then become so well acquainted, you get a feel for it.

RODGERS: But there's an art to it. Jim's one of the very best in the business at it. He's a quick study. He parachutes in, masters the subject very quickly, then he puts on an intelligent, comprehensive piece on the air for ABC on any given night. My hat is off to those guys. They're very courageous because sometimes they have to parachute into very dangerous places.

O'NEIL: I've often thought of myself as knowing a little bit about a lot, and a lot about nothing. As a generalist, I am comfortable with the role of being able to go into any situation, whether I've got 8 hours before deadline or 30 minutes before deadline. I present something on the air by deadline that makes some sense of what is going on, giving viewers at least a feel for what has happened on that particular day. It is a craft that you learn and that you develop over the years.

BURY: For a long time those of us in the bureaus were called firemen because when we would get the call, we would jump out on a chartered jet, land some place, do a couple of interviews, do the stand-up, run to the affiliate, rewrite some wire copy, and get something on the air. It's not great journalism, but it's got to be done, and all of us have done our share of it.

BITTERMANN: What we do about basing now confuses me in the post–Cold War era. Outside of the United States, most of our resources are in London. There is a little bit in Asia. Our European theaters have been pretty much closed down. You have to say, "Why do you want to put people in certain areas? Is it because you view the story as important? Is it because you get good transportation?" Transportation basing is not the best in London, but that's where we have the largest bureau.

RODGERS: But isn't that part of the Anglo-Saxon centrism? That plus the absence of linguistic skills?

BITTERMANN: Definitely. It's the language that does it.

FOOTE: Traditionally, nearly half of network domestic resources have been in Washington, and nearly half of the reports have come from Washington.

BURY: It's cheap and efficient to base a lot of people in Washington. Washington and New York have always been the two biggest production centers for the networks.

We do a lot of packaging now from Washington. For example, the Unabomber story for *Nightline* was covered mostly from Washington. Much of Waco was packaged in Washington and not Waco. We took in Unabomber reports from Montana, but we did a lot of interviews in Washington. Where we can find a few Washington elements, for reasons of costs they'll have the correspondent in Washington package it.

FOOTE: Is that a bad trend?

BURY: It's a bad trend if the story is reported in its entirety from New York or Washington. If you have a story such as the Freemen, I think you are much better served by having Roger O'Neil or our Denver correspondent on the scene. If it's a story that has elements and context from other areas, then it's not such a problem.

I think the Unabomber story was a good example where there were elements in Montana. There were Chicago elements because of Kaczynski's boyhood. There were New Hampshire elements. There were lots of Washington elements, though. In that case, I don't think it matters too much where it is you package the story.

In Harm's Way

FOOTE: Is there pressure on you to go into dangerous situations? Is saying "no" too many times the kiss of death for a journalist's career?

BITTERMANN: All of the networks have rules about if a correspondent feels something is hazardous, he can decline the assignment. But it does weigh on the minds of assignment editors. If covering news is part of your job, then you're supposed to do it. So, you just have to accept that.

I've often thought that the most dangerous thing we do is getting to the feed point on time. You are invariably rushing, and I have taken these hell-bent rides through the Iranian countryside or the Morocco desert that were absolutely dramatic. At times, you will be barreling down the road trying to make some deadline with a driver you don't know who claims to know the local driving rules. So, you just cross your fingers and say, "This guy is a professional," or at least we're paying him like one.

RODGERS: In the old days, we had to drive 80 miles an hour over snow and ice to get to the satellite point outside Moscow because the company was paying $5,000 for the bird. If you didn't make the bird, you were dead. There is that very real point that if you don't go to the war zones, I think there is a little invisible mark that goes against you.

O'NEIL: There was a time at NBC that the executives had a graph that they kept updated every month or so on airtime. There were nameless dots on the graph. Yet, it was very easy to know, if you watched the news, which dot belonged with which name. The number one dot on the NBC chart was our White House correspondent. The second dot was another fellow out of Washington. And those dots were used to determine whether or not the correspondents received new contracts or not.

FOOTE: At CNN, Christine Amanpour is being offered a large contract by CNN standards, presumably because she is willing to stay in the war zones.

RODGERS: But that's where the news is, that's where the story is, and that's where you go. As Churchill said, "There is nothing so exhilarating as being shot at and missed." And that's true, too.

BITTERMANN: I don't think that that's always where the story is. There are a lot of other things going on out there besides war and crisis situations. Part of our job should be to present the other side of things. Walt has the opportunity to do that because of CNN. But sometimes the broadcast networks get too fascinated with the idea that, if it's a crisis situation, it should be covered, and only crisis situations should be covered.

RODGERS: But it is the greatest adrenalin rush in the world. We came out of Afghanistan once, and we were in some hairy situations. I was on the ceiling for four days afterwards. I don't care if this generation uses drugs. Forget it. There is nothing like war for a high.

Lifestyle of the Correspondent

FOOTE: The lifestyle of a correspondent is touted as glamorous, but what about the travel, the transfers, the hours? Give us some insight on how you balance your personal and professional lives.

O'NEIL: Balance is the word. Many of us have not been able to do it very well, which is why many of us have been divorced more than once. My colleagues and I happen to be the exception. I've told my wife that my first love is my job, and she is number two. I said that seriously. I think she took it seriously and, for one reason or another, decided not to leave.

But in a very real sense, the job is my first love because I wear the beeper all of the time. I will give up vacations, holidays, birthdays, and anniversaries because it's what the job demands at this level.

From where I live and work now in Denver, there is no one else that I can depend on. If there is a story in my territory, I am the only correspondent.

But having said that, there are also rewards to this business that are very real. It is from the highs that Walter talks about to the highs of having an employer pay you a salary to see the world on their bill. I mean, what other job can you think of that allows you to travel throughout the world, rub elbows with presidents one day and bums on the street the next, and gain the kind of insight to what makes your country, or your world, tick, than the job we have?

None of us is in poverty, although all of us probably started in poverty. But it is a fairly nice lifestyle now. You can reward your loved ones with some monetary things for the sacrifices that they have to make. You also have the time off now when you have reached this point in your career where you can spend some real quality time with your family. I have a 25-year-old daughter who I chagrin to think grew up without me. But having said that, I probably wouldn't trade what I did to reverse that if I was given the chance to go back in time.

BURY: I think Roger is incredibly brave for telling his wife what he did.

RODGERS: Except it is true.

BURY: In any profession, there are real strains, but in ours, they can be extreme. If you get sent away to the Gulf War for 12 or 13 weeks, it's tough on your family. There are a lot of rewards, but it really is tough. Even before you get to the network in this business, you have to move five or six times. My wife was good enough to trail along with me.

It's tough to balance family and work. I have a teenage son. I feel real bad when I am out on the road because he is at the point in his life when I should really be around more. But when the beeper does beep, you have to go.

BITTERMANN: I dealt with the family pressure in kind of a peculiar way. I married my producer, which helped things out a bit. Through most of the 80s and early 90s, we traveled together. Last year, she left ABC to form her own company.

Our daughter grew up in France and is bilingual, bicultural, has two passports, and the whole thing. But for a long time, before she got into school, we brought her along on stories when we could. She saw the revolution in the Philippines although she was only two years old. We would bring along the nanny, and it was quite an entourage. The capability of doing that is limited these days, but it helped us to have a certain balance.

From the outside looking in, one might say, "Gee, that's great.

He's in the field. His wife is right there." But, it is just the opposite. When you're working with your wife all of the time, there is a certain strain there, being around the same person 24 hours a day. My wife highlighted it best by recalling the time that she was sitting in the bathtub and I rushed in and said, "Hey, have you got the phone number for the prime minister's office?" She said, "Well, where do you think I would have that phone number?"

So, there is a certain strain to it as well. You miss a lot of passages that you should be there for. I certainly have felt it being away at various times when I should have been home with my daughter. But the networks, especially ABC, are more understanding about trying to get you home for those big occasions. If you have a sick child or a sick wife or something, they're good about moving heaven and earth to get you back for that. But the rest of the time they expect you to go when the beeper goes.

RODGERS: It's all a trade-off. It's as glamorous as they say. My wife has lived in London, Berlin, Moscow, now Jerusalem. It's a wonderful life, but there is a price to pay for it. If you listen closely to what my colleagues said, it's the kids who pay the most. I have taken my kids skiing to Davos in Switzerland. We've Christmased in Florence, Rome, Paris, and all of those places. But in the end, there is something hard for a kid to have a visible parent, a parent who is in television. When they graduate from university, they might look at themselves and say, "I can't achieve that. How I can ever match it?"

FOOTE: Chris was sucked into a political campaign assignment that he thought would last a couple of weeks, but it lasted eight months.

BURY: I was doing what I thought would be a very typical show-ender piece about a pickle shortage when I was beeped. They wanted me to join the Clinton campaign in Atlanta. It was only going to be a short assignment until Super Tuesday, a couple of weeks later. But Clinton kept winning and winning. I didn't get home until after he was elected in November. I was home maybe six or seven Saturdays during those eight months. It was great to be on the national campaign and to see history in the making, but I missed a lot at home, too.

BITTERMANN: It is almost harder on single people in the business than people with families. We do have something to go home to. A lot of single people in our business get so driven because they have no outside life and no opportunity to develop an outside life. They're home for a day, and they'll start looking at the four walls. The girlfriend that they dated six months before is long gone with somebody else. The first thing they do is call the assignment desk and say, "Listen, is there anything coming up next week? I am at loose ends here." It may be tougher on them.

BURY: We have a lot of young single women at *Nightline*. Correspondents can go home at night if we are not on, but producers are expected to be there through the show, which is 12:30 A.M. The young women in our office call themselves "the *Nightline* nuns" because they don't have any real social life. It is five days a week until 12:30. Then they're so wiped out, they sleep until two o'clock on Saturdays.

RODGERS: I had a bright, young producer in Moscow who spoke fluent Russian and whose career goal was to go through Slavic studies, get to Moscow, then study, speak, live, work. She came at 25, and I inherited her on her second shift there. One night, she turned to me very weak and very teary-eyed, and she said, "Walt, I've wasted my whole life." From 25 to 36 years of age, she realized that she had been nothing but a machine grinding out news stories. She had wasted the best years of her life because we become so compulsive and obsessive about television.

BITTERMANN: One of the more unglamorous parts about working overseas is that you're working two sets of hours: New York hours and local hours. I've got a six-hour time difference from New York. Walt has eight. If I've got a satellite feed until twelve o'clock at night for New York, then I have to be back working French hours at nine o'clock in the morning. If it's a running story, that could be extremely tiring after awhile.

FOOTE: You really are an atypical group, all married, all with families, all with solid social lives. What advice would you give to the next generation of correspondents?

RODGERS: It is a tribute to the spouses that the relationship survives because it isn't us; we are very selfish people. It is sadly, tragically true. We are married to our jobs.

BITTERMANN: If you don't make enough time for the family aspect, you're distorting your view on things because most people are living in a family or a social arrangement that resembles a family. If you're this news junkie who goes from one port to the next, thriving on the news story, you're not really looking at the world with the same sort of take as someone who is representing the audience you're speaking to. I think you have to create time and make time for the family situation so you don't lose that perspective.

O'NEIL: As I've gotten older, the one thing I've learned is that I am really not needed to get a story on the air. Once I have written the story, I can turn it over to a producer, and I can go home. It becomes his or her responsibility to get it done.

It is the ability and the willingness to let other people do their jobs that they are eminently more qualified than you are to do; that allows you to get some semblance of order in your own life. I am doing more and more of that. The amazing thing that has happened since I've begun doing that is the migraine headaches have gone away.

FOOTE: But aren't we reaching all of you at a time in your lives where you are secure? You have made it to the top; you're clearly A-list correspondents at each of your networks. Would we have had different responses from you 20 years ago when you were insecure and just starting out?

O'NEIL: If anything, it is harder now for young people to achieve what we have achieved because my daughter just went through a job search in the field. Despite my wishes, desires, and urgings, she tried to get into this business and was having a hell of a time getting that first job, despite a college education. It wasn't because she wasn't qualified to get the first job. The new ingredient was the 5-year and 10-year veterans who were competing for the entry-level job as well because the dynamics of the business had changed so much. No longer can you go and seek the entry-level job and think you are competing only with people of similar background and education and experience. Now you're competing with someone who has had one or two jobs, has been laid off, and is just looking for any job. Because of downsizing across America, seeking the first job is eminently more difficult than it was for us.

FOOTE: Do you believe the perspective of a woman correspondent would be any different from yours?

BITTERMANN: I know some women correspondents who feel that they have cheated themselves by devoting too much time to career. Their biological clocks are ticking, and the ability to recover those years is a lot harder than for an older guy who suddenly realizes that he has lost something by being so crazed about one thing. So, I believe that their perspective would be even stronger towards the idea of making room for the family and personal life.

FOOTE: There are a third fewer of you in the correspondent corps than just 10 years ago. Where have these folks gone? What are they doing?

RODGERS: They are probably very happy.

BITTERMANN: They have weekends.

BURY: Some have set up their own production companies; some have gone into government. I know quite a few who are press spokesmen. So, there is life after the network. I think all of us are probably fearful of what it is, but it is out there.

FOOTE: What would each of you be doing if the network correspondent's job came to an end tomorrow and you were hitting the streets, writing a resume, and looking for a job?

BURY: I suppose I would try a go at freelancing. It's the one thing that has always differentiated print from broadcast. There has never been a really steady corps of freelance writers and reporters in broadcast the way the magazine business has them. With all of the outlets now and all the cable stations, I suspect that you could probably eke out a decent living doing things for cable.

BITTERMANN: That's a little bit of what my wife has found out in the few weeks she has had her production company going. There are a lot of outlets out there besides the networks these days. There is evolving the possibility of freelancing as a producer or as a correspondent. We have freelance soundmen and cameramen. There is a whole cadre of freelance producers in Europe. I am not sure to what extent they exist in the United States. Now we have several regular contributors to ABC who are freelance correspondents, Hillary Brown, and others.

It goes back to what I was saying earlier about absorbing everything you can because the kind of correspondent you may have in the future will be somebody who can feel absolutely comfortable on the Internet. As a producer you might want to design Web pages for the Internet one week or do a segment for the Discovery Channel the next. In every industry, you must be very flexible and adapt.

O'NEIL: What got me in trouble in the first place in this business was my voice, so I suppose I would continue to stay in trouble with that voice by renting it out and doing, God forbid, commercials, if I had to. But there's good money in commercials, so what the hell.

As with photographers and technicians, companies would rather have you as a freelance employee than as a staff employee. I was amazed to learn that it is 33 percent cheaper to hire a freelance crew than it is to have a network crew on staff because of all of the fringe benefits. The freelancers that I know make a lot more money than they used to. They work probably as much, but they also have the ability not to work if they don't want to, a luxury you don't have if you're staff. *Dateline*, which is now on four nights a week with more than 100 staff producers on the payroll does not have any staff photographers or soundmen; they are all freelancers. So, there is a brave new world out there of freelance, where you work for whom you want, if they want you.

Typical Workweek

FOOTE: How long do you work each week?

O'NEIL: Generally speaking, I am working 60, going on 70, hours a week. And it used to be 50, going on 60. So, it is getting worse. I expect that to worsen again with the addition of MS-NBC.

My bureau chief managerial duties probably take 10 percent of my time. The extra time that I am working is on stories, on the demands of the various shows. When you're done with *Nightly News,* then you have to worry about the morning programs. If the morning programs think it is worth a live shot, you not only have to rewrite a core spot for *The Today Show,* you have to be up at four o'clock in the morning to do the live lead-in and the live tag. So, on a busy news day, you're running 18-, 20-hour days. Generally speaking it's a minimum of an 11-hour day.

BURY: I think probably about 60 hours a week is fairly average. We start our day at *Nightline* with an eleven o'clock conference call. The show goes on the air at 11:35, and we do a fair amount of same-day crashes.

On the days when I don't have a story, I can go home early. If I am caught up in a breaking story, like Roger, then the days are obviously much longer. But it's not atypical for us to have one story completely finished and then get assigned another one late in the day.

The day of Ron Brown's plane crash, I had just finished writing a six-minute piece about six o'clock. My boss came and said, "Do you have the Ron Brown piece done?" I said, "Yeah." He said, "Great because you're doing the Unabomber story tonight." So, I turned around and wrote another six-minute piece for the show that night. That's the kind of thing that we do a lot.

BITTERMANN: Overseas, it's a little bit different because it comes in spurts. About 60 to 70 hours a week is probably average. We are contractually obligated to be available 24 hours a day, seven days a week. There is never really a downtime when you sort of feel like you can relax.

When you get a breaking story, that's when it really is telling because you are forced to follow up things continuously for all shows. You're almost always the only person available in that location. So there is nobody to come in and spell you for, you know, *The Today Show, GMA (Good Morning America),* or *Nightline.* A 36- or 48-hour stint without sleep is not unusual on a breaking story, especially when you initially arrive on a story.

RODGERS: In the Middle East, even when you have these great stories that die down, CNN is so omnivorous that the next day it's a sausage factory. "We want another spot on something else," and it goes on and on.

I am, more weeks than not, in the office seven days a week. The hours are the same, anywhere between 60 and 80, but let's say an average 70-hour week. I am in the office at nine unless there is an eight o'clock call. I am never out of there before nine at night. You're constantly going. I think ABC is brilliant because years ago they made a decision that the correspondent would never be the bureau chief.

At CNN they go just the other way. It is very difficult to do both jobs well. Being a bureau chief in a high visibility post like Jerusalem, everybody calls in and wants to talk to the bureau chief, and it is exhausting.

Then there are dozens of job applicants. You have got to constantly deal with them; plus you've got to worry about the story and cover it. The key to success is having a good staff, but it is still terribly tiring. You're always on that electronic leash.

You know, the high point of my day is if I can get to go to the YMCA and work out for an hour.

O'NEIL: The high point of my day is if people don't come in and ask the questions. People truly want to be stroked. The baby-sitting is unbelievable.

BITTERMANN: And there is a phone version of that, too. I get this constant harassment from New York and other places where they'll be calling in and wanting to know this or that. There is a memo version of that where you have respond to memos that come in. That whole off-air thing can be as time consuming as the on-air thing.

The Perfect Network Would Be . . .

FOOTE: What would you change about network news?

BITTERMANN: Get more people in the field; get them out of the major centers, in our case, New York, Washington, and London. Some of those personnel could be used better in the field as news gatherers.

Every dime is accounted for nowadays. Taking a taxi across town has to be assigned to a program. I am not so sure that that is a very good idea when it comes to gathering news. The positions that one needs to do all of that accounting could be better spent if you turned them into news-gathering positions.

BURY: For a long time, I was the only correspondent in Chicago, often covering a huge section of the country. That's clearly not a wise use of resources. I would look at the correspondent roster and see there were 30 correspondents in Washington. And there I was covering 22 states. I would reinvigorate the bureaus, distributing correspondents and producers outside of New York and Washington. The second thing that I would like to see is longer reports—at least two and a half minutes for a network report. Fewer reports of greater length and perspective would be nice.

BITTERMANN: I have always thought that a minimum for a report with any kind of texture or context to it is one minute forty-five, preferably two-thirty. But the average report from overseas is around one-thirty, one-fifteen maybe.

O'NEIL: The texture and the feel that the executive producers say they want is loud and clear at ten o'clock in the morning when they give you two-fifteen or two-thirty for a report. When they do the line up in the middle of the afternoon, they still want the texture and the feel, but now you're back to two-ten. When they really get to the final rundown, you're back to two minutes. And by the way, they also want you to add this and that. It is putting a round peg in a square hole. It doesn't fit. So you take out that texture and the feel, and you have just another regular run-of-the-mill report. What makes you different is that texture that you had to cut out.

BITTERMANN: Absolutely. That's what people remember. They don't remember the voice-overs of wallpaper as we call it.

RODGERS: The news business has become a prisoner of a star system. Give it back to the reporters. Let the reporters get back into the news business. There's been a retreat from the news business, some of it towards magazine shows, some of it towards the star-cast system. Once you go back to what you were in the business for to begin with—news—we will straighten out some of the wrongs.

If I had to change anything at CNN or CNNI, I would ask for greater editorial scrutiny because sometimes some sloppy and downright wrong things get on the air. We lose some accuracy in the quest for immediacy. That may be unavoidable, but as an old news hack, I still like to see "Get it first, but get it right."

Contributors

Jim Bittermann joined CNN as Paris correspondent in 1996. During and immediately after Princess Diana's death, Bittermann was the backbone of the CNN coverage. He served as Paris correspondent for ABC News from 1990 to 1996, covering the turmoil in the former Soviet republics, the liberation of Kuwait, the American humanitarian mission to Somalia, and the negotiation of the PLO-Israeli Peace Agreement in Tunis and its subsequent signing in Washington. Prior to joining ABC News, he was European correspondent in Paris for NBC News for 10 years. In 1988, he received a National News Emmy for his work covering the 1988 Sudan famine. Bittermann received his bachelor's degree in journalism from Southern Illinois University at Carbondale. (Photo courtesy ABC, Inc.)

Chris Bury has been a correspondent for ABC News *Nightline* since 1993 and has covered many major international and domestic stories, including Whitewater, the American military policy in Haiti, the political battle over health care reform, and the siege of the Branch Davidian Cult in Waco, Texas. Bury joined ABC News in 1982 as a general assignment correspondent in Chicago. In 1983–84, he reported on the Democratic and Republican National Conventions, George Bush's vice presidential campaign, and the Gary Hart presidential campaign. During the 1992 presidential election, Bury served as the *World News Tonight* correspondent covering the Clinton campaign. Bury is a 1975 political science graduate of Southern Illinois University at Carbondale. (Photo courtesy ABC, Inc.)

J oe S. Foote is the dean of the College of Mass Communication and Media Arts at Southern Illinois University, Carbondale and the author of *Television Access and Political Power: The Networks, the President, and the Loyal Opposition*. Before entering university teaching, Foote served as press secretary for Speaker Carl Albert and administrative assistant to Congressman Dave McCurdy. Foote is past president of the Broadcast Education Association, a member of the Accreditation Council for Education in Journalism and Mass Communication, and a recipient of the Frank Stanton Fellowship from the International Radio and Television Society. Foote is a graduate of the University of Oklahoma and the University of Texas. (Photo courtesy Southern Illinois University at Carbondale)

J ohn S. Jackson III is a professor of political science and the provost of Southern Illinois University, Carbondale. His teaching and research specialties are political parties, party leadership, presidential elections, and Congress. He is the author of *The Politics of Presidential Selection* and, with William Crotty, of *Presidential Primaries and Elections*. His work has appeared in the *Journal of Politics, American Politics Quarterly, Polity, Midwest Journal of Political Science, Western Political Quarterly*, and *Legislative Studies Quarterly*.

M ichael Murrie is an associate professor and director of the Telecommunications Master's Program for the Department of Radio-Television at Southern Illinois University, Carbondale. Murrie is a contributor to *Television Broadcast* and the *Communicator* specializing in television news technology issues. In addition to more than a decade of academic experience, he has 12 years of experience in television news as a reporter, photographer, assignment editor, and producer, primarily at KSDK in St. Louis. He earned his master's degree in journalism from the University of Missouri at Columbia and his doctorate from Southern Illinois University at Carbondale. (Photo courtesy Scott Kemmerer, Southern Illinois University at Carbondale)

Roger O'Neil has been the NBC News Denver bureau chief and correspondent since 1983. He was the lead reporter for NBC during the Oklahoma City bombing trial of Timothy McVeigh and has reported on a variety of domestic stories, including the dramatic Yellowstone fires and numerous environmental issues. He joined NBC News in 1979 as a Chicago-based correspondent. Before coming to NBC News, he worked for NBC affiliates in West Virginia, Kentucky, and Texas. O'Neil is a 1969 graduate in radio-television from Southern Illinois University at Carbondale. (Photo courtesy NBC, Inc.)

Walter C. Rodgers joined CNN in 1993 as the Berlin correspondent and currently serves as bureau chief and correspondent in Jerusalem. Prior to joining CNN, Rodgers worked for ABC News for 12 years, serving as Washington correspondent and Moscow bureau chief/correspondent. Rodgers has covered the U.S.-Soviet presidential summits, the assassinations of Israeli Prime Minister Yitzak Rabin and Martin Luther King Jr., the Chernobyl nuclear disaster, and the Iranian hostage story. Rodgers has also written for the Associated Press, the *Washington Post*, the *Christian Science Monitor*, and the *Washingtonian Magazine*. Rodgers received a bachelor's degree in 1962 and a master's degree in 1964 in history from Southern Illinois University at Carbondale. (Photo courtesy CNN, Inc.)

Marlene Sanders, a three-time Emmy Award–winning correspondent, has broken barriers for women throughout her career. While a correspondent at ABC News in 1964, she was the first woman to anchor a prime-time network newscast. In 1976, she was the first woman to become a news vice president at the networks when she was named vice president and director of documentaries. After 14 years at ABC, she joined CBS News for 10 years. She also spent 3 years with PBS in New York, anchoring *Profiles in Progress*, an independently produced series of documentaries shot in the developing world. She taught at Columbia University's Graduate School of Journalism and is now with New York University's Department of Journalism. She is also a professional in residence at the Freedom Forum's Media Studies Center. She is the author, with Marcia Rock, of *Waiting for Prime Time: The Women of Television News.* (Photo courtesy Joe Pineiro, Columbia University)

George Strait has been ABC News' primary correspondent on medical and health news since 1983. He contributes to *Nightline* and *World News Tonight with Peter Jennings* on AIDS, health care reform, and the medical and ethical concerns regarding new technologies. In 1995, for the second time, Strait received his industry's highest award, the Alfred I. duPont Award, for a ground-breaking series on women's health. He led ABC's coverage of South Africa's transition to democracy in 1994. Strait has received a Gold Medal Award from the National Association of Black Journalists and a Blakesely Award from the American Heart Association. Strait earned his bachelor's degree in biology from Boston University and his master's degree in biochemical genetics from Atlanta University. (Photo courtesy Steve Fenn, ABC, Inc.)

Ed Turner is CNN's first editor-at-large, representing CNN News Group globally on editorial matters, including seminars, speeches, writing assignments, and network guidelines on accuracy and fairness. Formerly executive vice president responsible for CNN's news-gathering resources, Turner covered the 1991 Soviet coup, the war in the Persian Gulf, and the 1989 crisis in China. He was vice president of news for Metromedia, Inc., vice president of UPITN in New York, and producer of *CBS Morning News.* He holds a bachelor's degree in broadcast journalism from the University of Oklahoma. (Photo courtesy CNN, Inc.)

Garrick Utley is a contributor to CNN from the network's New York bureau. Before joining CNN, Utley served 3 years as ABC News' chief foreign correspondent. He also spent 30 years with NBC News covering international affairs and reporting from more than 70 countries. Utley received the Overseas Press Club's Edward R. Murrow Award for his reports on Soviet-American relations and in 1986 was given the George Foster Peabody Award for his contributions to "Vietnam: Ten Years Later." Utley holds a bachelor's degree in political science from Carleton College in Minnesota.